THE LIONS DIARY

THE LIONS DIARY

JEREMY GUSCOTT

AND NICK CAIN

MICHAEL JOSEPH

LONDON

MICHAEL JOSEPH LTD

Published by the Penguin Group
27 Wrights Lane, London W8 5TZ
Penguin Putnam Inc., 375 Hudson Street, New York, New York 10014, USA
Penguin Books Australia Ltd, Ringwood, Victoria, Australia
Penguin Books Canada Ltd, 10 Alcorn Avenue, Toronto, Ontario, Canada M4V 3B2
Penguin Books (NZ) Ltd, 182–190 Wairau Road, Auckland 10, New Zealand

Penguin Books Ltd, Registered Offices: Harmondsworth, Middlesex, England

First published 1997

Copyright © Jeremy Guscott, 1997

Set in 11¼/15½ pt Monotype Joanna
Typeset by Rowland Phototypesetting Ltd, Bury St Edmunds, Suffolk
Printed in England by Clays Ltd, St Ives plc

A CIP catalogue record for this book is available from the British Library

ISBN 0 7181 4313 2

This book has to be dedicated to my wife Jayne and to Saskia, my daughter, who was born whilst I was on tour with the Lions. Also to the whole of the Lions playing squad and management plus everyone who truly believed we could win the series. Enjoy.

CONTENTS

Prologue   1

1   Cotton Connects   17

2   Touchdown in South Africa   25

3   Border Deluge   35

4   Pussycats or What?   43

5   Doddie's Demise   59

6   Gored by the Blue Bulls   75

7   Seeing Off the Lesser Lions   95

8   Netting Sharks in Natal   105

9   Cape Crusaders   115

10   A Drop for the Dead Donkeys   133

11   A Bridge Too Far   147

Epilogue   155

Appendix 1: The Squad   159

Appendix 2: Tour Record   189

ACKNOWLEDGEMENTS

Thanks to everyone involved in putting together such a great book in such a short space of time – especially Nick Cain, the co-author, who had to translate everything I said into plain English, and everybody at Michael Joseph/Penguin for turning everything around so quickly.

THE LIONS DIARY

PROLOGUE

Typical, people said, of all the drop-goals, in all the world, it had to be you.

If you'd seen me spraying drop-kicks all over the pitch in training during the previous week – off the outside of my foot, off the inside of my foot, off the end of my toe – you would have bet as much money on me putting it over as you would on a one-legged man in a backside-kicking competition.

Did I know it would go over? No. No way. I had already sent one scudding wide about a foot off the ground in the first test. So why, of all people, with the score tied at 15–15 in the second test, three minutes of normal time left to play, and a historic series win for the Lions at stake, did it fall to me to do the honours?

Because I was there. As Fran Cotton would have said, 'Simple as that.' Much as I might have felt like the wrong man in the right place,

I was there, with the eyes of the 55,000 souls crammed into King's Park, Durban, drilling into my every movement.

The moment is frozen in time in my memory. Probably because freezing was what was most on my mind. As the ball drifted towards me through the arc of the floodlights everything seemed to happen in slow-motion. I dreaded its arrival. What if I missed? How had it happened?

I knew the answer to the second one: we had lifted the Springbok siege and had started to counter-attack strongly in the last 10 minutes of the match. Woody had hacked the ball down the left-hand touchline as the massive Lions contingent roared him on in the Durban night. Gregor Townsend had then darted for the line but was hauled down inside the 22. Scott Gibbs drove in to help clear the ball at the ruck. The target was in our sights.

I had stepped inside to the fly-half position and knew that we had no chance of an overlap on the outside with two of our backs already committed. When the ball came back to Matt Dawson he shaped to pass straight behind him, but in an instant he looked at me. There was panic in his eyes – and probably mine too – but he realized what was on and managed to swivel round and get the ball away to me. It had to be done.

I knew where the posts were so I didn't have to look up. I concentrated purely on putting boot to ball and kept my head down. I prayed it wouldn't miss. I prayed it wouldn't be charged down.

I struck it cleanly. The sense of elation I felt when I eventually looked up and saw the drop soar between the posts will stay with me for ever.

The Lions supporters went ballistic, and the boys on the field heaped congratulations on me, but there were five minutes remaining in which we had to protect that 18−15 margin. Five minutes before the 1997 Lions, the first professionals, wrote their name large in British rugby's hall of fame. When the final whistle went, Fran Cotton found me with a bear-hug which nearly broke my ribs. If he had, it wouldn't have made a jot of difference, because I was on such a high I was anaesthetized.

I couldn't believe it. We had won against the odds against the most arrogant rugby nation on earth. We had made history. All I wanted to do was soak up the atmosphere, to drink in something that would stay with all of the 1997 Lions for the rest of our lives. I also wanted to share it with my family and friends. After the press conference was over − you couldn't have wiped the smile off my face even if I'd been forced to eat a lemon − I phoned my wife Jayne at home in Bath with our three daughters, Imogen, Holly and Saskia. Saskia had been born while I was in South Africa and I had only seen photos of her for the first time that morning.

There was a hug from my mum, Sue, who had come out to South Africa for the tests, outside the dressing-room, and then I called my dad, Henry, back home in Bath. After I scored the match-winning try for the 1989 Lions in the second test in Brisbane he had been so pumped up that he walked down to my house, which was being refurbished, and smashed down a partition wall in about 30 seconds flat. He was so excited he said, 'This time I don't know whether to cry or be sick.'

After that I called my two lifelong mates from back home, Chalkie Wardell and Pete Blackett. I got Pete on the phone. There had been nine of them watching the match in his flat. A mate, Nathian Simms, had popped round to Pete's when there were 10 minutes to go and said, 'Could you imagine if that bleeder drops a goal to win the game?' When they knew it was me on the end of the phone they went mad.

In retrospect, I'm pleased that I was there to kick the ball. Pleased for the family and friends who had stuck by me through thick and thin, and for all my colleagues, players and management alike, on the 1997 British Isles tour to South Africa, and for the supporters who did us proud. Not only that, but pleased for the Lions, and for myself for having had the privilege to play for them.

There is nothing in rugby to touch the Lions. They have always meant more to me than any other team. Lions tours are far more intense than playing for England – they provide a stage on which you can find a place in history. They certainly provided me with a world stage on which to play a leading role after an unpromising season with England in which I had had to play bit-parts.

For me the 1996/97 season was the proverbial roller-coaster: it began with a dip in fortunes, but ended on that unbelievable high in Durban following my selection for the Lions tour. In between it was, in an England context, a bit of a pain in the backside because I spent most of the time extracting splinters from mine after spending the season on the bench.

During the Five Nations I managed the princely total of 43 minutes on the field and after England's last game of the campaign against Wales I thought, 'I don't know if I could sit on the bench again.' A few moments later I thought, 'Well, maybe I could,' but you don't realize quite how frustrated you've been until it's all over. I suppose I won't know for sure until I'm asked again. Against Ireland, although a lot was made of the three minutes Austin Healey and I were on, the hard work had already been done. I took the euphoria with a pinch of salt. The Welsh game was different. When I saw that Jon Sleightholme was in trouble, my heart sank. Wing was the last place I wanted to go on, because you feel so exposed. I'd played there for Bath eight years earlier and hated it – I've done nothing worse in rugby. So I went over and told him he couldn't come off and tried to gee him up, but when he told me he couldn't see out of his left eye I knew the game was up – and I was on.

Once on the pitch, I didn't think too much about it. Whatever decisions I made in defence I made quickly and stuck by them, and when I got the ball I decided I was simply going to run into space. As it worked out things went extremely well, but give me centre any day. It was a charmed 40 minutes. I'd helped set up two tries – Tim Stimpson's and Richard Hill's – even if I felt like a scared cat running purely on instinct.

However, while all's well that ends well, the early signs last season were not good. During the summer a provisional England squad had been announced with a number of the old lags – myself, Dean Richards, Rory Underwood, Brian Moore, Will Carling, Jon Callard, Graham Dawe – all omitted. It amused me when I saw the form come through from the England management saying that we had been omitted on the grounds that they knew what we could do. How that made us any different from any of the others in the squad with 10 or 15 caps – presumably they also knew what they could do – is totally beyond me.

However, that sort of approach is something you come to expect from the RFU, so at the time I did not see it as a great setback and nor did it made me think, 'Oh crumbs, I'm determined to play really well this season just to prove people wrong.' It was just something I accepted. I'm one of those people who believe that there's no use crying over spilt milk and my approach was not to play rugby with any more thought or determination than normal; it was simply to continue to play in a way that I enjoy most.

Obviously one of the main factors in my being relegated to the bench by England was the appointment of my Bath colleague and centre partner, Phil de Glanville, as captain of England. At the club myself and other guys like Adedayo Adebayo and Jon Sleightholme used to take the mickey out of Phil when he was mooted as a prospective candidate for the England job. It was all light-hearted stuff: I used to say to him, 'The only way you're going to get the England job is if you are captain, because there's no other way you're going to get in,' and Phil used to smile in his knowing sort of way. Deep down Phil is very, very competitive and a strong-minded individual. In many ways the banter coming out was good because it dissolved some of the tension. It was also typical of the sort of humour we have at Bath. It may seem fairly vicious to outsiders but, believe me, by our standards it was pretty tame.

The day before it was announced officially, he was on a golf course with 'Sleights' and Jon Callard – as soon as Sleights had it confirmed, he was on his mobile phone to the bookies trying to get a slice of the action but none of them was interested – but I already knew because Phil had phoned me up and said that Jack Rowell, the England coach who had made his name in the glory days at Bath, had made him captain. I congratulated him there and then, but I realized immediately that it was now a straight race between Will Carling and myself for the other centre position. If I'm honest, based purely on the way I'd been playing I thought I'd get the nod. I considered that it would also be in my favour that I'd been playing centre where Will had been playing fly-half and had only had two or three games at centre. A further factor was that I'd been playing outside centre for England and Bath where Will normally played inside centre.

As soon as Jack Rowell called me I knew I had lost out to Will, because he had no other reason to call. 'Hello,' said Jack, and I thought, 'Oh yeah, it's you.' I was silent because I know Jack well from his years at Bath, and I know he always likes to put the onus on others to do the talking. He said, 'We've picked Will.' I maintained my silence. He said, 'What are you doing – counting up to ten?' I think my answer was along the lines of 'more like a thousand'. And guess what? There and then, I couldn't be bothered to ask him why. The way I saw it, the decision had been made in selection and, disappointed as I was, no amount of explanation over the telephone was going to make me feel any better or change the situation.

Later that day I got a lift to training with Mike Catt, Jon Callard, Sleights and Phil de Glanville. Phil, who has an input in selection but no vote, had an inkling that I was out, because Jack had bounced it off him and then, as is his way, gone away to have a rethink. In most instances the rethink doesn't change anything, and I admitted to them that I'd had the phone call from Jack. Phil apart, the boys couldn't believe it. Phil, who was in a no-win situation, said, 'So that's the way he's gone – never mind.' What else could he say?

When we got to England training at Bisham Abbey, Will and I looked at each other and shrugged, as if to say, 'So that's the way it is.' I wasn't the only disappointed man at England training that day – Kyran Bracken had been ousted in favour of Andy Gomarsall – but my disappointment was different because I was an experienced player being dropped by his country for the first time. I can't measure it against the other setbacks I've had in life because, quite simply, I don't tend to dwell on them, I dismiss them as soon as possible. But I do remember being surrounded by the massed ranks of the rugby media and vowing to myself, *Terminator*-style, 'I'll be back.' It certainly wasn't going to be the end of my England career, I knew that much. However, you have to be dignified when you're left out of a side, because if you go the other way you look pathetic.

One thing that stands out in my mind is when Rob Andrew was dropped a few seasons ago in favour of Stuart Barnes for a Scotland game and he said that he was going to have to have words with the then England manager, Geoff Cooke. I can recall wondering at the time just how those words were ever going to affect the decision that had been made. Incidents like that make you stop and think about how careful you have to be in what you say to the press. I knew that there would be a commotion as to why I'd been left out, but I had time to mull over what I was going to say to them on the drive up to Bisham. The obvious course of action was to take it on the chin, and not denigrate anyone else, but make it clear that I had no intention of throwing in the towel.

The most difficult question to answer was the one they all asked: 'Has Jack told you why he left you out?' As you know, I hadn't asked him when he made the dreaded phone call. Subsequently, throughout the autumn games I was hoping that the moment would come when

I could say to him, 'Come on, give me the real reason why you left me out.' That moment never arose, and to this day I don't know all the whys and wherefores. Some of the steam was also taken out of the issue by Jack saying that he wanted to see how it worked out and that he would take stock of the de Glanville–Carling pairing after two games. So there was a little crack of light, but also a question mark in my own mind – and for me this particular question mark was hanging over Phil rather than Will.

At the time Phil was the best choice for the captaincy because he already had a strong rapport with the coach, and his main rival, Lawrence Dallaglio, had very little international experience. The other candidate was Jason Leonard. 'Jase' is a good friend of mine, but the only problem with having a prop as captain is that you can lose momentum when you need it most. This was apparent in the game against Argentina, when we needed direction when the chance came to take quick penalties – the only problem was that Jase was often buried at the bottom of a ruck. It's difficult for a front-row forward to be at the hub of the game giving quick signals.

However, there is no denying that Lawrence Dallaglio was the best England player on the field throughout last season. Whether he would have been the same player if he'd been given the captaincy – well, I'd have to say probably more than likely. So the gamble of giving the captaincy to someone as inexperienced as Lawrence might have paid off, and it might have allowed me to continue my England career without a hiccup. That's all all right with hindsight, but it doesn't blind me to the fact that when the decision was taken Phil was the obvious choice.

De Glanville is quite a tough nut, and he's had to be, given the stick that came his way over the course of the season. For me 'Hollywood' is just another Bath player – i.e. someone you take the mickey out of – and nothing changed in that respect after he was made England captain. For instance, when he turned up to training after England's defeat by France, Richard Webster, our Welsh flanker, dubbed him 'the 60-minute skipper'. He, Jack and I have history – although I wasn't really involved: during the 1995 World Cup, Phil gave Jack a really hard time when there were suggestions that I was off form and that he should be given his chance. I can understand his frustration because he had been on the bench for two seasons. Now I've been on it for one, and when I gave him a hard time he told me, 'You just keep that bench warm.'

Phil was under pressure in the media for not being worth his place. At one stage he even stopped reading the press, but he kept himself going unbelievably well, and I admire him for that. He took a lot of stick and never spat the dummy. After the season he's had, this next year will probably seem like a cakewalk.

As for Jack's decision to pick Will ahead of me, he could argue the pros and cons for either of us as players convincingly. In fact, on one occasion, he did. He said that over the previous two seasons a comparison between the two of us gave Will the edge because he was stronger than I was in contact situations. That's not something I'd disagree with because Will has always been good at taking the ball up, staying on his feet in contact and providing a target for his forwards, but it's all a matter of horses for courses, and if that's the game you decide to play, fine. However, if you are talking about opening up and expanding your game, as Jack was, I think my record shows I am able to do that. Many pundits were of the opinion that Will and Phil played similar games, and that you needed a different sort of player as a foil.

Whether these playing considerations weighed more heavily than 'political' factors is another question. I don't suppose we will ever know whether Jack weighed up which axing would cause the greater furore. What I do know is that as a former Bath coach he was conscious of laying himself open to accusations of Bath favouritism, and another Bath player in the England backline could be one too many.

In a professional sporting environment that sort of thing should not matter a damn, people should have the courage of their convictions. Jack's convictions were to leave me out – but let's not get this out of proportion. What I would hate is for things to deteriorate into a schoolyard slanging-match. There's been too much water under the bridge for us to start treating each other that way. I have to try to

understand his decisions even when I don't have a huge amount of respect for them.

I wasn't the only one who was a little baffled by Jack's decision to leave me on the bench, however – a point that seemed to be underlined when I was picked as a centre for the Lions squad. This meant a huge amount to me in what was a difficult season. It would have been easy to see it as a kind of 'I told you so' to Jack, but that was never the case. I was overjoyed to be going with the Lions to South Africa, pure and simple. This was always going to be my last opportunity to turn out for them, and nothing else really compares.

I've probably got another couple of years of top-flight rugby left. In fact, my contract with Bath was due to expire at the end of the 97/98 season, but I enjoyed myself so much last season that we agreed to extend it for one more. However, it's pretty flexible. For instance, if I didn't play particularly well the club would be in a position to call it a day, or if I decided I wanted to finish at the end of the 97/98 season, I'm sure they'd let me, given the close nature of my relationship with them.

As far as my England future is concerned, it will be very interesting to see what happens next. The new coaching team has got a few things to work out. Will Carling may be out of the running, but there is no shortage of midfield contenders. Before he was concussed badly towards the end of the Lions tour, Will Greenwood was playing very well, there's Phil, and I'm still around. Who knows what comes next? Having shifted from outside to inside centre at Leicester, Will Greenwood has come on in leaps and bounds, while Phil de Glanville finished the season in good form with Bath after getting progressively better during the Five Nations.

In the end it all depends what the coach wants from his outside centre. Does he want someone who can finish off what's been created on the inside, or does he want what he had before? Let me put it this way, I'm not holding my breath. Life's too short to eat yourself up worrying about things that are outside your control. Mind you, there's no way that at 21 I would have thought that way, but because of the exposure I've had over the intervening ten years I'm able to put things in some sort of perspective. For example, the biggest change in my life has been nothing to do with rugby; it's been getting married and becoming a father. Those things are far more important than rugby, however much you love the game.

All I want from the game now is not to play too much rugby that I don't enjoy – and if that means having to play the sort of game England were playing three or four years ago then I would definitely walk away from it.

In my rugby life, when I was 21 my only goal was to play for Bath, and once I'd achieved that I thought I'd done enough. Well, I hadn't, but since then something of that 'everything else is the icing on the cake' attitude has stayed with me. I didn't have a clue that I would end up playing for Bath for ten seasons, let alone for England. And that I would have the ultimate honour of playing for the Lions, in not one but three test series – against Australia in 1989, New Zealand in 1993 and South Africa in 1997 – had not even entered my wildest dreams.

Chapter 1

COTTON CONNECTS

The phrase 'talk softly but carry a big stick' could have been written for Fran Cotton. I've rarely met such a huge man with such a quiet voice, but anyone who made the mistake of thinking that he would tread the boards lightly when he was appointed manager of the 1997 British Isles touring side to South Africa was soon made to think again.

It seemed that no sooner had I bumped into Fran after the first Bath v. Leicester game of the season (our second game of the season) when he asked me about my availability – I told him that I had always been a great supporter of the Lions concept, and always would be – than he was embroiled in controversy.

The first signs of friction emerged when Will Carling said publicly that he had turned down the Lions captaincy before the long squad of 65 was announced. Fran jumped straight in and refuted the claim, saying that he had asked him only about his availability and that Will had asked him for the captaincy. If Will said that, then that's between him and Fran. When Will denied Fran's version, you got to the stage where the debate was being conducted in the papers and you got the silly situation where no one knew who to believe.

Too much of the selection process seemed to be conducted in the press, and the timing of the announcement of the long squad just prior to the Five Nations definitely did not help matters. The captaincy issue and the furore over the non-selection of Phil de Glanville were two cases in point. I don't know why Fran felt it necessary to keep on stating the criteria for the captaincy, because he put himself in the position where the press were going to keep on asking questions and he was going to have to keep answering. In Phil's case you will never know what was said unless you were there, but ideally speaking most of what was said between them – i.e. Fran was never going to select me – shouldn't have gone to print. I know that Fran went down to Bath to see Phil to knock any misunderstandings on the head, but by then the damage was done.

So, by the beginning of April, when the final squad of 35 was picked, I have to admit I had some reservations about the manager. However, where the balance of the squad was concerned, I thought the selectors had done a very good job, bar the inevitable three or four selections where everyone will always argue the toss. The only problem was that the harder I looked at the list, the more I realized there were a lot of players I had hardly met beyond playing against them once or twice.

That state of affairs was soon remedied when the squad was invited to assemble at the Oatlands Park Hotel, Weybridge, Surrey, on 11 May to prepare for the assault on South Africa only days after we had finished the longest and hardest season in the history of British club rugby. Before the 1989 and 1993 Lions had departed British and Irish shores there had been at least a couple of training weekends before we assembled, whereas we had a week and were then straight into South African conditions.

Because this was one of the shortest ever preparation times available to a Lions tour party the management had decided to take a short-cut to team-building by inviting the Impact Training Group to put us through our paces. Impact may have worked with such big name companies as BT, Barclays, British Airways and Sony, but when they introduced themselves to the squad the overriding attitude towards them was one of scepticism. Rugby players are not the most receptive audience to new-fangled ideas you could find, but Ian McGeechan played an important part in getting the Impact group accepted at our first squad meeting. Geech made the point that this tour more than any would require people to have open minds and be flexible, and that we must accept what was thrown at us.

I shared the scepticism. I'm a bit old-fashioned about these things and, as far as I was concerned, a quick drink down the pub would have been enough for me to get to know everyone. It's easy with the benefit of hindsight, with the tour a great success, to say it all worked a treat, but there were definite differences of opinion at the time. However, what is also true is that we all took Geech's words on board and buckled down to our Impact lessons.

We were split into groups of eight or nine – a mix of players and management, different countries, different positions, the long, short and tall – and asked to balance a long bamboo cane on the end of our fingertips and, all together, lower it to the floor. Now that took co-ordination – so it took ages to get right. We soon discovered that any exercise we did would then be subjected to group analysis with our instructor. In our case he was a rather deep bloke who seemed to think there was some hidden psychic truth in what we were doing. 'What did you feel?' he asked. 'A piece of bamboo,' we replied. By the time he had gone round everyone in the group trying to find out how he could speed things up, the old concentration batteries were running a bit low.

For the rest of it, it was *Krypton Factor*-type stuff. There was a crate-stacking exercise with the objective of building as high a stack as possible with one of your group perched on top, some canoeing and a brain-teaser involving two canisters of water and a scaffolding pole. It was like being kids again. The regression to childhood – which I didn't object to – was made complete when we were all given our little patch out in the back garden at Oatlands and handed the raw materials to build a catapult from which we fired wet sponges at our rival groups.

However, once we'd decided to give it a go, everyone got stuck in and, in the groups I was involved with at any rate, no one stood out as any kind of brains trust. Mind you, that was hardly surprising with blokes like Doddie Weir around. When he tried to take over the group, it didn't take more than a couple of exercises for the rest of us to work out he was clueless. Result? Doddie would say what he needed to say and the rest of us would ignore him and get on with getting it right.

In the end the Impact lessons had more pluses than negatives because the squad took them on board and gave them a good lash. Whether it got us together as a group any quicker than rugby training would have done, I'm not sure. It was a diversion, and it affected people in different ways, but, as I've said, I'm something of a cynic – as one of the Impact boys discovered. I was sat down at one of the big tables having lunch with Scott Gibbs and Ieuan Evans. I gave a deep sigh and said, 'What are we doing with those clowns from Impact this afternoon?' Scott looked at me and said, 'You'd better ask him, because the clown's sat just down there.' I looked down to the end of the table where one of the Impact directors was quietly eating lunch. Talk about shooting yourself in the foot.

I wasn't that negative, and we had a laugh doing some of the exercises, but there were times when we were doing the analysis that

I thought I'd rather be in my room getting a couple of hours' kip. However, if only I'd known that that was the easy bit. The most difficult bit of the whole Weybridge get-together was yet to come: establishing our own 'Code of Conduct' for the tour. It took twenty-four hours of mental graft and was incredibly intense.

This consisted of working out how we were going to live our lives for the next seven weeks. Training, playing, discipline, the lot. In retrospect, it was the most sensible problem a group of rugby players has ever been set. Rather than be told by others how we were going to behave, the responsibility was thrown fairly and squarely in our court. It was certainly a novel idea for the Scots lads because the previous summer, on their tour of New Zealand, Jim Telfer had cracked the whip and imposed curfews here, there and everywhere. If he had tried it on a Lions tour, it would have backfired like an old banger.

As a result of the 'Code of Conduct' I began to see Fran Cotton in a different light because, as manager, it was his call. Instead of dictating he took the view that these were grown men who could work things out for themselves. We came up with a twenty-point code which, for example, laid down no rules about alcohol. Our attitude was that if someone was used to having a glass of wine on the Friday night before a match that was his prerogative. But it's amazing in those circumstances what peer pressure does and consequently, throughout the tour, if someone was playing on a Saturday the chances of him having a drink after Wednesday were virtually nil. We also decided that once a week we would go out as a squad and do something together, either go out for a meal, or out to the cinema or out to watch the Harlem Globetrotters as we did in Durban.

Chapter 2

TOUCHDOWN IN SOUTH AFRICA

Having stepped out of one press conference on to the plane, our first port of call in South Africa was another one courtesy of South African rugby's 'Mr Big' – big in a rugby sense means big in every sense in South Africa – the SARFU (South African Rugby Football Union) president, Louis Luyt. I'm not a political animal but I know enough to know that he is every inch the dictator and that nothing gets by in the South African game without his fingers having touched it or eyes read it. Whether that's going to last we'll have to wait and see, but I doubt it very much.

Despite the fact that our destination was Durban we all trooped off the plane at Jan Smuts airport, Johannesburg, for the presidential welcome – 'Welkom to Sarth Afreeka' – except it was a lot longer than that, what with a 16-year gap since the previous Lions tour and the chance to cream the Brits 3–0 to make up for their earth-shattering defeat by the All Blacks 12 months earlier. You couldn't help but think, when Louis said, 'Brilliant to have you here and the bist of luck for the tist series,' that it was as loaded with irony as a 12-bore, given that the bookies were giving 5–1 against us winning a single test and most of the media pundits were also predicting gloom and doom – but more of that later.

The formalities over, we then trooped on to another plane and winged our way towards hot and humid Durban to prepare for our first match, against Eastern Province six days later. No sooner had our feet touched the ground in the land which spawned Shaka Zulu than we were into a training regime which would have made even one of his impis wilt.

With the temperature at 80 degrees or more we sweated blood. Initially we would go through five or six basic drills all designed towards achieving greater continuity. For example: first, one guy running out and placing the ball on the ground whilst falling, second guy picks up, steps over, goes five yards and does the same. Second, one guy falls and places the ball, two more drive over and a third picks up before the sequence is repeated. Third, same process except this time the third man pops the ball to a fourth player running along the side. This sort of variation was repeated for another couple of phases until we reached the ideal, which was every player going, turning, popping, going, turning, popping. Now that might sound as if we were all on 'E' – all the rage in the new South Africa – but, take it from me, this was no rave.

That lot constituted the warm-up and took about 15 minutes. Then we were into the serious stuff. It was eight versus eight, the attacking side wearing contact suits – strategically padded jerkins which still allow a full range of movement – the defending side ordinary training gear, applying the skills we'd warmed up with to match conditions with opposition and tackling. We'd do these sessions for two hours or so, and I found them not only hard but boring.

I don't mind the eight versus eight deal as long as it's short, snappy, and quick, i.e. attack for two minutes, turn around, defend for two minutes, and get it done. What I dislike is when it goes on . . . and on . . . and on. The hardest thing for me is that coming from Bath I'm used to going into training sessions where we know we're doing this for 10 minutes and that for 20. In that sense Bath have taken a leaf out of the New Zealand way of doing things, whereas with these Lions we went on until they said, 'That's it' – but you never knew when that would be.

Part of the problem was that the two Scottish 'Bravehearts' who coached us quite literally eat, sleep and drink the game. Not to put too fine a point on it, we were being coached by the two biggest rugby obsessives in the British Isles. Consequently the word 'tired' does not feature prominently in the vocabularies of either, and they had a pretty old-fashioned view of training. Both Geech and Jim seemed to have missed the point that, where it may be all right to flog schoolboys because they know no better, any player who has been around the houses at international level is a slightly different proposition.

Having said that, there were management meetings every night and three times a week the senior players from the various countries were involved in those, so the messages about how the players were feeling should have been getting through.

Maybe I was in a minority of one, because after a few days moaning about it I realized that it didn't seem to be sinking in with any of the others, so I stopped and got on with it. When all is said and done, although I was at odds with the training regime, nobody wants to be known as the tour whinger and we were playing for a common cause.

The Tuesday night before the side for the first game was announced, myself, Lawrence, Scott Gibbs and Jason had been out for a late one at TJ's ('Thunder Junction') nightclub at King's Park thinking it'll be just our luck to be called up tomorrow. We were all there as Fran was reading out the team list, fingers crossed that we were going to be surplus to requirements. All of our names came out of the hat, followed by a few dodgy looks between me and my fellow revellers. In the end, Scott missed the game because of a twisted ankle. For the rest of us there was no escape. In truth, I was looking forward to the game and to having Will Greenwood, the only uncapped player in the squad, as my centre partner because his form for Leicester during the season had been very impressive and, who knows, I may even get the chance to partner Will in an England shirt. The only other adjustment, and a more serious one, was getting used to Gregor Townsend's very flat alignment because we had been playing deep at Bath all season.

In fact, I was glad to have been selected to play in the first game because we had been training so long without firing a shot in anger, and I was happier being out there than having to sit and watch the proceedings whether or not we played well or badly. I wanted to get going and put the preparation to good use. I was surprisingly anxious and I had that weird feeling that I often get before big occasions which can be best explained as a 'what the hell am I doing here' feeling. That was counteracted by the sense of just what a momentous event this first professional Lions tour was in anyone's career, whether they were 19 or 32.

Saturday, 24 May: British Isles v. Eastern Province

When we took the field at Boet Erasmus – or Telkom Park as it had been unlovingly renamed – we really didn't know what to expect. Given all the hype there was even a hint that we might get blown away, but we were so much in control after 15 minutes that I thought we were going to run away with it. Unfortunately, like most scratch sides, we made too many basic errors either side of half-time to totally impose ourselves and we let them back in.

For a first-up performance – admittedly against one of South Africa's weaker top provincial sides – this wasn't a bad effort, and in the final quarter I felt we could score almost at will.

Obviously I was also delighted to score the first try of the tour, although most of the hard work had been done before Gregor's long 'miss-one' pass found me in the gap with their three defenders outmanoeuvred. They were never going to get anywhere near me and all I had to do was run between them. My second try in the second half was simply a question of supporting Will Greenwood's break and running it in.

I said in a piece for the *Evening Standard* well before the tour started that we were being badly underrated. Even give or take five or six differences of opinion over the best Lions starting line-up, given our best fifteen against South Africa's best fifteen there was no way I was ever going to accept that we were going to be beaten by anything like 20 points a game or three tests to nil.

I couldn't believe how pessimistic people – and the media in particular – were being about our prospects. Eastern Province might not have been the strongest side around but Luyt had made sure he stiffened them with the inclusion of two Springboks from their 'twin' province, Gauteng, in the shapes of lock Kobus Wiese and centre Hennie Le Roux (there was also a strong suggestion that he was cracking the whip over those two players because they were in contractual dispute with him).

In the final analysis a scratch Lions side beat Eastern Province comfortably, and even though we experienced a few difficulties in the scrummage, we came through strongly to win the match by playing running rugby. Now, I'm no scrummaging expert, but I know enough to know that when one pack is backpedalling they're getting the worst of it, and there is little doubt that we were back-pedalling at the scrum. Consequently I wasn't especially surprised when the South Africans, with Eastern Province hooker and skipper Jaco Kirsten as the mouthpiece, tried to steal a psychological march after the match by claiming that our forwards were less physical, and less powerful, than southern-hemisphere packs.

Let's face it, the South Africans are obsessed by scrummaging. The traditional way for a young warrior to prove his manhood in the Masai tribe in Kenya is to kill a lion. The equivalent South African macho display is to prove that you're strong enough to scrummage a bulldozer backwards when it's in first gear. They still base so much of their game on macho scrummaging it's untrue. As a result they made the mistake of thinking that just because our scrummaging wasn't going particularly well at the outset the rest of our game was weak – and we made them pay for it. Talking to the front-row boys afterwards they were of the view that you are always going to have teething problems and it takes being confronted by the opposition to know where you've got to tighten up. Overall I felt like saying to Kirsten and co., 'Hello, South Africa. This is rugby 1997 style, and you're out to lunch.'

What really got my goat was not the South Africans and the early propaganda war but the British media reaction to the result at the post-match press conference. Having scored two tries, I was asked to attend. Sometimes it's hard to know just what they're on about. All they seemed to be able to focus on was the negatives, i.e. that neither the scrummaging nor the opposition was supposedly up to much, with barely an acknowledgement that the Lions had, in most respects, performed creditably in their opening engagement of the tour.

The overall tone was one-eyed and pessimistic and you sensed that they almost couldn't wait to see us slip up and confirm their worst suspicions. The joke, however, was on the media, not least because in most instances their pre-tour test selection predictions were so far wide of the mark come the first test that most of them would have been lucky to have got half the line-up. I couldn't believe just how naive and negative they were, and it was a recurrent theme for me throughout the tour.

I'm often asked – and the Eastern Province press conference was no different – what sort of a buzz I get scoring tries, but the honest answer is that there are not many that make you think, 'Wow!' It all depends where and when and what has gone before, and, let's face it, there are not many perfect moves or tries. The match-winner in the second test against Australia in 1989 is pretty well the only one that has given me immense satisfaction, but I haven't done that since. There are none as vivid as that, although I live in hope!

My priorities have changed. I have always become frustrated if I don't get enough ball, but whereas in the past I used to compensate by trying to do too much when I eventually received it, now I am more patient. That said, if neither myself nor the wingers see enough ball the simple rule as far as I'm concerned is that we are not playing the game as we should be. Getting the ball is a major part of my enjoyment in rugby, and if I don't see enough of it I get hacked off.

Generally speaking, as with my first try against Eastern Province, you see the space well before you get the ball. So when you get your hands on it you're wondering if the gap is still there to exploit. Usually it is. However, there's a distinct difference between arriving in the space without the ball and then receiving it and sliding through, and running with the ball to create the opening. Running without the ball is freer because you're running into space, and so you shouldn't get touched. When you have the ball and have to beat people you are on autopilot. It's instinctive, like having sensors. You know, almost as if you have sonar, that if you continue heading one way you will be closed down so you change pace, direction or both.

Off the field it was a pity we didn't spend a little more time in Port Elizabeth, because it is the home town of my (at that stage absent) Bath team-mate, Mike Catt, and I would have liked to spend a little more time with his family. I had a phone call from his mum on the morning of the game wishing me luck and inviting me round for a Sunday lunch I couldn't make because we were moving on. But I did manage to meet up with his three brothers, Peter, Richard and Douglas, for a drink when, after an unmemorable meal at the local O'Hagan's, South Africa's Irish pub/restaurant chain, we finished up celebrating at a local night spot called Cadillac Jack's. Douglas's wife had just had a baby and it was her first time out socializing for months. After she'd had a few drinks she started tucking into me about being away from my wife when she was having a baby. A few years ago I might not have hesitated to answer back, but being a little more sensible and mature about these things than I used to be, I sat back and took it all and tried to be a little more understanding.

In the meantime the Lions had a point or two to prove as we headed for the armpit of South Africa, otherwise known as East London, for our second match.

Chapter 3

BORDER DELUGE

Not the most exciting place in the world, East London. We didn't get off to the best of starts when, after waiting for all the other passengers to get off the plane, we bypassed all the baggage formalities as usual and got straight on the team bus; however, no sooner had we driven out of the airport than the bus conked out and we all sat around for half an hour waiting for a replacement. When we eventually got into town I thought we must have taken a wrong turning. There was nothing to East London except for a number of stock South African institutions: a beach front, lots of unemployed black men, an O'Hagan's, South Africa's Irish pub/restaurant chain, a Holiday Inn – where we were billeted – and, heaven be praised, a Health & Rackets club. One of the welcome breaks provided on the tour was the excellent chain of Health & Rackets clubs throughout South Africa, of which we were made honorary members for the duration. They had state-of-the-art gyms and good indoor swimming pools and had the great bonus of getting us out of the close confines of the squad into a different environment with different faces; a very necessary change of scene.

The second mishap was that I was down to share a room with Keith Wood. He's a lovely bloke is Keith, but he snores for all Ireland. I lasted one night but then had to call on the services of my mate Jason Leonard to take over the night shift with Woody. Jason managed to sleep through it where I couldn't. There are few things I find more irritating than snoring. I just can't shut my mind off to it. I know I'm a bit of a hypocrite because I rumble a bit myself after having a few beers, but I don't have to listen to that.

I was a member of the Entertainments Committee – along with John Bentley, Scott Gibbs and Doddie Weir – which tried to liven things up by organizing some golf and go-karting, perhaps a trip to the cinema, but the reality was that the main reason the tour was pretty boring in comparison to '89 and '93 was that you were so tired from training it was hard to raise a gallop when it came to other activities. On a typical day you would train in the morning, have your lunch by two, then have a couple of hours off resting before a team meeting at six – and by five, being their winter, it was dark. The measure of the tour socially was that one of the most popular pastimes was watching films on video, so one of the first things we would do on arriving at the next town would be to sort out a deal with a local video store. Like they say, too much work and no play – and I don't mean rugby – makes Jack a dull boy.

The only problem was that, professional as we were in one sense, getting fed on the Saturday after matches was already proving quite difficult. After the Eastern Province match we went to eat at a place called Toby Joe's, and the combined efforts of Jonty, our SARFU liaison, and Bob Burrows, the Chardonnay Kid, didn't stop us waiting until 9.30 p.m. before we got served. Bearing in mind that most of us had not eaten since mid-morning and had played a match in between times, you can understand why they caught a bit of flak. Our humour wasn't improved by the fact that we were stuck there at a prominent table like goldfish in a goldfish bowl, while everyone around was partying and cat-calling to us. That, to borrow a phrase, do I not like.

The side for Wednesday's game against Border, one of South Africa's poorer main provincial sides, was announced on Monday and was immediately followed by a big contact session. It was during this that we had the first internal training spat when Ronnie Regan and Barry Williams had a difference of opinion during scrummaging practice. Given the way the press latched on to Williams's supposed head-butt you could have been forgiven for thinking that World War Three had just broken out. It was no surprise to us because it's just one of the by-products of competition for places you get in clubs and national teams, so why not with the Lions? It was only a matter of time and who it was going to be – and the front rows in opposed scrummaging sessions are the most obvious flashpoint.

Fran Cotton put it in its proper perspective when he told the press: 'For the first couple of hits we didn't really have the outside control of simulated refereeing that we would have liked and there was a clash of heads, and that's what caused the flare-up. I don't think there's anything of note, and the two protagonists have had a good chat and a laugh about it. It's not really an issue.' Asked if he approved of head-butting in training Cotton joked, 'It's good for the mental toughness of the team.'

The backs were not mere spectators. We had a fiercely contested contact session of our own in which no quarter was asked or given, and after it was over none of us was left in any doubt that if you went in half-cock you weren't going to do yourself any favours.

Then, on the morning of the game, it was the turn of the non-playing side to get a bit of a beasting from Jim Telfer. I wanted to get his measure, so I decided to give him a bit of the cheeky schoolboy treatment. I kept on telling him that he was in danger of losing his touch if he thought he was putting us through a rough old session. He took it all on board and bided his time. Then, at the end of the session, he put us on the tackle bags and I knew it was payback time. Where everyone else did 10 tackles each my name kept on cropping up and I ended up doing 17 or so. That was our first session of mind games and Telfer had no hesitation in making it physical.

Jim and I didn't have a proper chat throughout the tour. It's probably just as well because where rugby is concerned I don't think we sing from the same hymn-sheet. He's very much a forwards' coach, and anything outside that he relies on video for his analysis; in fact he's almost a rugby video junkie. You may already have gathered that I'm not a great one for videos. I've always played my rugby – and, in many ways, lived my life – on the basis of touch, feel and instinct. For Jim, who has spent the last three years cooped up in an office as Scotland's director of rugby rather than coaching, it must have been like a new lease of life to get to South Africa and thrash the living daylights out of the Lions.

Wednesday, 28 May: British Isles v. Border

There was a simple lesson learned in East London: irrespective of how hard you train, play the game the conditions dictate. There had been a deluge for about 24 hours prior to the match and the pitch at Basil Kenyon stadium was waterlogged. So waterlogged that it prompted this classic juggling of headlines on the front page of the local rag, the *Daily Dispatch*.

The main four-deck block headline was 'Lions Match – Worry Over Waterlogged Pitch', while at the bottom of the page there was room for a much smaller story with a single-deck headline stating 'Mandela Assassination Threat Uncovered'. Unbelievable if I hadn't seen it with my own eyes.

On with the match – although most of the guys who played might have wished otherwise with the gift of hindsight. The side, captained by Rob Wainwright, made the mistake, when it was wet, of trying to play the type of game we aspired to ideally in dry conditions. There was a further complication when it became apparent towards the final quarter that, when we needed to kick, Paul Grayson was unable to do so because of the recurrence of his groin injury.

Consequently we made hard work of an ordinary side which, cheered on at every turn, grew in stature as they took confidence in our difficulty in clearing our lines. From where I was sat in the stands, a further disadvantage was that we got off to such a cracking start. Given how large John Bentley had loomed over the early part of the tour – Bentos is an upbeat, noisy Yorkshireman, who was the only Lions rugby league returnee not have played in the five Nations – it was fitting that on his first appearance in a Lions jersey he scored with his first touch of the ball.

It all seemed so easy. Scott Gibbs made the incursion, Allan Bateman ran a great angle before offloading to Tim Stimpson and his pass to Bentos saw him stretch over in the corner. The match was two minutes old.

After that we tried to do too much and they cashed in on our mistakes. We made it very hard work for ourselves, and in the end, after Ronnie Regan had forced his way over, it was left to Wainwright's try off a driving maul from a lineout seven minutes from the final whistle to turn around a 14–13 deficit and save the day. If Border, who had plenty of spirit, had been a little more inventive they might even have snatched a famous victory – but they didn't, and they were beaten three tries to one as the Lions came through in the final 15 minutes.

Within the squad our confidence wasn't shaken at all. There was disappointment that our second scratch side of the tour had not shown what we could do because of the conditions, but it certainly wasn't heads down or low morale because of the performance. After all, we had won and we knew we had a lot more ammunition than we had fired. Everybody had been in games at club level when you haul yourself out of the mire to win, and, as has always been said of Bath, it's the sides who have the habit of winning when they have played badly who are the ones to watch out for.

Chapter 4

PUSSYCATS OR WHAT?

In the wake of the Border result the South African press decided to go to town on our perceived weaknesses, i.e. up front, where we had twice struggled at the set scrum against lowly provincial opposition and where our play in the loose was seen as less 'robust' than that of southern-hemisphere sides.

The *Cape Times* led the way with a match summary under the headline 'Lions starting to look like pussycats'. In it the Border scrum-half, John Bradbrook, a New Zealander, took up Kirsten's cry from the Eastern Province game that we lacked physical presence – but he went a few steps further. 'They were soft, both going into the tackle and in the tackle situation. South Africa will be making a big mistake if they don't take these guys on up front,' said Bradbrook.

'I tried to hassle their back row and scrum-half a bit. It seemed to intimidate them and, even on the occasions I took the tackle, it never felt like I had been pumped back in the contact. They appeared to shy away from head-on contact. That, more than anything, surprised me,' he added.

Anything you say, John. Nothing is a better motivator than being bad-mouthed by the opposition and when, thankfully, we left the wet and windy 'Wild Coast' of East London for Cape Town there was an overriding sense of frustration that we had barely scratched the surface of what we were capable of. Consequently, I thought the 'pussycats' tag was pretty naive stuff, but then we all know that there's very little humility around when it comes to South Africans and rugby.

That the unfinished business was going to be attended to first in the Cape of Good Hope had a nice ring to it. I'd been to Cape Town twice before – once, briefly, for the World Cup semi-final débâcle against New Zealand and then for ten days last year shooting the final of *Bodyheat* – and had liked it very much. Of all the places in South Africa it was the one with the sense of things being closer to what we know back home. Things like trees lining the roads, people walking along the pavements, a few old-looking houses you warm to because so much else in South Africa seems either to have been built for purely functional reasons or is hidden by a wall and barbed wire and is guarded by security men.

South Africa must lead the world by miles in terms of security men per head of population – which tells you all you need to know about the crime statistics. I remember hearing during the 1995 World Cup that in Johannesburg there were an average 65 car-hijackings a day, and now it's even worse. Not exactly the sort of thing that makes you want to tell the family to go and pack their bags and head for a holiday in sunny South Africa. In any case, my wife Jayne had spent time in Durban and Cape Town during the World Cup with my daughters Imogen and Holly and didn't feel that secure.

However, I felt comfortable with Cape Town. It was unlike the rest of South Africa, which seemed so big and yet so empty. You felt as if somebody needed to get hold of the place and just shake it, and maybe people and a bit of life would come tumbling out. I couldn't get over how empty all the city centres were. Durban, for example, was like a ghost town compared to cities in the UK – even in Bath during office hours the place is teeming by comparison.

One of the drawbacks with modern touring compared to the old days is that it is all a lot more impersonal. There's no way you can build lasting friendships when you're only in a place for three days before you move on, or a week if you're lucky – or unlucky. In modern rugby you're cocooned in the safety of your hotel. It's a bit like being in a comfortable prison where you stay to preserve your sanity and protect yourself from overbearing outside demands. Fans are a case in point. Let me say first that I realize that spending time with the people who support you comes with the territory if you are a high-profile sportsman and it's not something I begrudge. But someone somewhere will always want a minute of your time. Unfortunately what they don't realize is that for us it's their minute

. . . followed by another minute . . . followed by another and another and it can add up to a hell of a long time.

I guess much of the modern touring experience can be summed up by this: I've been to South Africa three times now and never been near a game park. However, the flip side of the coin is that there is no way I'd be happy with a three-month tour. Now it's professional, the best it's going to get is a six- or seven-week Lions tour like the one we were embarked on. National squads on tour don't compare with the Lions, or certainly not in my experience with England. The mix of talent from the four home unions and the tradition associated with the Lions cannot be replicated by a single country. To be brutally honest, you're not playing with the same quality of player. This is the best the British Isles has to offer, and that makes it unique.

This time, what made it even more unique was the inclusion of the rugby league returnees, the two Scotts, Gibbs and Quinnell, Allan Bateman, Dai Young, Alan Tait and John Bentley. Of the lot, Bentos was by far the most vocal – particularly on the training field. Having made his mark against Border, Bentos was subsequently selected for the Saturday game against Western Province, who, despite a dip in fortunes last season which resulted in them missing the cut for the Super 12, are still seen as one of South Africa's 'big four' provinces.

He was on something of a high, and given that he'd been a former beat bobby in the run-down Hyde Park area of Leeds where he had to tackle bad lads on a regular basis, he was looking forward to confronting James Small, the Western Province and Springbok winger who had cultivated the image of being the bad boy of South African rugby.

That made us partners for the first time, because I was also given my second run of the tour. On the training pitch in Cape Town one of the first things that struck me about Bentos was just how much banter there was flying about. But it had a serious edge, because Bentos wanted maximum involvement. He was trying to call moves here, there and everywhere. Now, if you try and do that from the wing it's generally considered to be tantamount to committing suicide. Because Bentley had been playing rugby league for eight years he was used to a highly structured game, where there are set moves and not too much variation. Anyway, it didn't take me long to remind him that at Bath we had a saying that wingers are seen but not heard, and that he should go and park his backside on the touchline. Although he promptly told me to eff off, I'd made my point.

On the field I struggle with people sometimes because a lot of my rugby is natural, instinctive, call it what you will. When things get too regimented, it simply doesn't work: the chemistry is not there. But Bentos wanting the ball was the least of my concerns – a far greater one was learning how to play off Gregor Townsend, an instinctive playmaker.

One of the things that I was careful not to do was to lace into my partners too much if they made mistakes in the same way I would if

I was training with Bath or England, because I think it would seriously have stuffed some of them up mentally, Gregor not least.

Gregor is a very gifted player, a natural and instinctive talent, but he also has the concentration span of a gnat. At fly-half you are 'The Man', the dictator, you're saying how it's going to be played. If you're not totally focused for eighty minutes you make mistakes – and if you make mistakes you lose games.

We trained at Villagers, which is an old Cape Town club side based near Newlands, and the setting, with Table Mountain looming in the near distance, is spectacular. At this stage in the build-up to the match the sessions were not too physically demanding in terms of contact, but they were long in terms of the time spent out there and the concentration required. The repetition factor was so great that by the end you were mentally drained. However, I wouldn't say that my sentiments about training were mirrored right across the board. The guys from Scotland or Northampton who had worked with Geech since the 1993 Lions tour knew what to expect, as did the Leicester boys who were used to long sessions with Bob Dwyer. Basically, if you were used to spending two and a half hours on the training field it wasn't a problem. But if, like me, you were accustomed to one and a half hour sessions, it was a chore. I suppose the root cause is that I get easily bored, and repeating the same thing day-in, day-out is as stimulating to me as watching paint dry.

In the end, as a rugby professional, instead of putting mind over matter you often have to put matter over mind. The struggle is more against losing interest than it is against not putting in the effort or not wanting to do well.

You may think I'm being a bit over the top about training, but it was such a major element in the life of the 1997 Lions squad that it merits a caliper test every bit as exacting as the ones Dave McLean gave us.

A typical day consisted of breakfast at 8 a.m. followed by a squad meeting in the team room at 9.15. We would be on the bus to the training ground at 9.30 and generally start warming up at 9.45. Training would last until at least midday and it was rare that we were back at the hotel before 1 p.m. Then you would have a shower and lunch between 1.30 and 2.30. The next couple of hours were free for you to do whatever you wanted, but you needed to get cracking because, it being the South African winter, it started to get dark at 5 p.m. Then, if you were a forward, you would probably have a meeting because Jim Telfer was such an enthusiast he often wanted to get the boys into the classroom for some homework. Subject? How to beat the Boks. Generally, from 6 to 6.30 we would meet as an entire squad for a video session. At the beginning it was to watch South African Super 12 stuff and it would last anything from 30 minutes to an hour. Once we started playing matches this evolved into match analysis and the video sessions became targeted more at team groups. At 8 p.m. we had supper and after that the lame, sick and lazy got tended to by 'The Doc' and masseur, Richard Wegrzyk, alias 'The Painless Pole', while the rest of us painted the town red (in our dreams).

Mind you, I've got better at touring as time has gone on, especially where it comes to living out of a suitcase. I used to pig it. Jayne packed my bag so well before I left that the only person who could repack it would be her. I was so bad that, whenever we had to move on, it would take me a couple of hours to gather my kit up from all corners of the room. I used to make the mistake of leaving all my gear in the bag – thinking it would save time – and then dig in at will and create real mayhem. Now I always unpack, put folded clothes in drawers, shirts on hangers, shoes in wardrobes etc., and, hey presto, when it comes to leave and put everything back in the bag, it fits perfectly. I've learned the hard way that being organized and systematic makes for a far easier life and, as a knock-on, I try to be as punctual as possible and make a point of not being late for team meetings.

Being organized paid dividends in particular on travel days when we almost always trained in the mornings before a midday departure. Usually this resulted in a Houdini-like escape from the hotel which involved showering and packing within 45 minutes of returning from the training ground. For the most part we moved around with the minimum of fuss, and there was the bonus of none of the flights within South Africa lasting any longer than a couple of hours. That said, Stan Bagshaw, our appropriately named baggage master, probably saw things quite differently as he chased up missing items of kit from all over the country. Stan was a real brick throughout, and one of the hardest-working of a support staff which for the most part applied itself off the field as hard as we did on it.

The usual form on the flights was that, while most of the squad slept, unhindered for the most part by autograph hunters, a card school formed around Austin Healey, Matt Dawson, Ronnie Regan and later Mike Catt. They made sure that the slumber was not uninterrupted as they howled at each other's misfortune when money passed from one hand to the next.

What was also apparent as we moved around South Africa was just how important this tour was to the people. Everywhere we went the welcome was fantastic. It amazed me. The respect for the Lions and their tradition was immense, not least because of the unbeaten tour in 1974.

The reaction from the general public was one of warmth and sincerity, and, unlike at the World Cup in 1995, they were not desperately trying to oversell the place. Then, if I heard 'This is God's Country' once, I heard it a thousand times. This time they seemed far more self-assured. They were more interested in you, what your hopes and ambitions were as Lions, than simply you being interested in their country. The only thing that took me a while to get used to was the way, whenever anyone wanted to attract my attention, they used to refer to me as 'Hey, Guscott!' Back home if someone uses your surname rather than Jerry or Jeremy you immediately think, 'You cheeky sod', but in South Africa it was the norm.

In fact, name-calling seemed to be the order of the day in the early part of the tour and, as the 'pussycats' tag indicated, it was by no means all from well-intentioned fans. It was to flare again as the Lions addressed the business in hand – a solid win over one of South Africa's leading provinces.

Saturday, 31 May: British Isles v. Western Province

Fran Cotton reminded us before the match that, if we beat Western Province at Newlands, one of the benchmarks of the tour would have been successfully cut. To win at one of the spiritual homes of the South African game, in Danie Craven territory, would, we were told, begin the process of undermining the Springbok fortress. Consequently, by the time we took the field at Newlands we were itching for action. We were getting a bit tired of hearing about Western Province's great tradition and how they were the best non-Super 12 opposition we would meet en route, as the local press predicted, to getting stuffed in the test series.

In one sense it was a strange game, because the question marks raised over our scrummaging ability grew bigger rather than smaller. However, we compensated with a powerful display in the loose and, with the England flankers Lawrence Dallaglio and Richard Hill prominent, we made a number of turnovers and won the bulk of the possession on offer.

There is no denying, though, that our scrum creaked badly. The Western Province front row of Garry Pagel, Andrew Paterson and the veteran Keith Andrews, all of them Springboks, gave Graham Rowntree, Barry Williams and Jason Leonard a hard time and, given the amount of disruption, we did well to take an 18–14 lead into the second half.

Despite our 'local' difficulties, I am a huge supporter of the new law requiring the back rows to remain bound to the scrum until the ball is out. It has given the game, as well as scrummaging, a new lease of life. It has simply opened up the game by giving backs more space off first-phase ball, and has made attacking scrummagers worth their weight in gold. An unstable scrummaging platform on your own put-in makes life much more difficult for your backs to get over the gain-line. It also reduces your options significantly, i.e. in deciding which flank you will attack, if your pack is unable to turn the scrum and keep their back row away from you.

Although we went into reverse at the first two scrums, in all other respects we started convincingly and Martin Johnson, making his first tour appearance, had every reason to feel pleased. We were only denied an early try when Ieuan Evans lost possession in the act of going over but Tim Stimpson, who proved in this match with a tally of four penalties and three conversions that we had more quality goal-kickers in the squad than had at first been supposed, converted the pressure into points with his first successful kick. Then, after 14 minutes, a sharp break by Gregor Townsend gave me the opportunity to put Bentos over in the corner and we were on our way. So was Bentos. It was first blood to him in his private battle with James Small – but there was more, much more, to come . . .

Overall the match was frustrating because I saw so little ball. I must have touched it all of six times. Of all the provincial sides we played, 'Province' were probably the most inventive. They offered variations on the battering-ram approach adopted by most of the others and, like us, tried to play open rugby. They also had in Andrew Aitken, a compact no. 8, and Dick Muir, their captain and inside centre, two focal points. It was no accident that Muir, who makes up for not being the quickest centre with his creative skills, scored twice in the first half from well-worked blind-side moves off scrums. But by then we had scored again after Gregor, myself and Bentos – who again got past Small – had put Alan Tait in for our second try.

Although Western Province went ahead briefly, 21−18, early in the second half with a try by Brink set up by Aitken, I never doubted that the Lions would win. In the end WP did not have enough all-round fire power to clean us out and, even though they were a quick side prepared to move it wide, overall they could not take us for pace. I was not surprised when, after a couple of Stimmo penalties had restored the lead to 24–21, we ran in two more tries in the last 12 minutes, the first by Ieuan but made by Rob Howley's break, and the second by Bentos – his second of the afternoon – from a hack ahead by Richard Hill just before the final whistle.

Bentley was, of course, cock-a-hoop on three counts: the Lions had won, he had scored twice and he had won his personal duel with Small conclusively. At that juncture I was totally unaware that there was any bad blood between them. You're so wrapped up in the game that you're not generally aware of vendettas between other players.

However, while Johno's post-match reflections included such gems as 'That was tougher than anything I've ever experienced in the Five Nations, full stop,' and Muir responded with 'I didn't expect the Lions to play as fast a game and I was impressed by their handling skills,' Small was busy laying into Bentos – verbally.

Upset by Bentos's 'sledging' – apparently it's quite normal in rugby league for people continuously to abuse each other – and having not only had a brief tussle on the touchline in the second half, but also seen his opposite number score twice, Small refused to shake Bentos's hand after the match was over. Asked why, he started singing to the South African press. Once more we were front-page news for the wrong reasons as Small alleged that, during their little altercation, Bentley had gouged him in the eyes.

'I have no problem with what Bentley said to me on the field, I also said things to him,' commented Small. 'Players swear at each other all the time – it's nothing new. But what he did was not within the rules of the game. He fingered me in the eye when I was defence-less. I took exception . . . and that is why I did not shake his hand. I thought the act was cowardly,' he said. And to make matters worse, according to the Small version of events, 'He ran past me screaming: "It was me . . . it was me!" '

Small's account – like his rugby career – sounded a little too much like the script from a soap opera for my liking. Certainly 'The Pink Salmon', alias Fran Cotton, was having none of it. 'The accusation is total nonsense. It's an attempt to deflect attention away from a pretty average game and the fact that Bentos scored two tries down his wing. We're not here to massage James Small's ego,' said Cotton. That sounded about right to me, and it obviously didn't cause the WP coach, Harry Viljoen, any sleepless nights because he confirmed that they would not be citing any Lions players.

For my part, verbal abuse on the rugby field simply doesn't register. It goes in one ear and out of the other. I don't react verbally to verbal abuse on the rugby pitch – and I can't remember the last time it happened it was so long ago. Actions speak louder than words, and I'm happy to let them do so. As for the Bentos and Small saga, while I support my team-mate and think he did well to out-psych Small and get the better of him, it doesn't blind me to the fact that Bentos is the more mechanical of the two players. Small is a natural footballer but, in the WP match, he only managed to show it once. He had six yards in which to move. He went inside, then out, around Bentos, and chipped on. He was too far out to do damage but, had he been 20 rather than 35 metres from the try line, he might have scored.

Chapter 5

DODDIE'S DEMISE

Looking back on the Western Province game I can't say that I was delighted with my own game, and a hangover after a night spent celebrating at the Cantina Tequila in Newlands and a nightclub called Sirens didn't improve the perspective. I like to come off the pitch feeling fulfilled, having had as many opportunities as possible and made the right decisions at the right time. Generally, the more ball I get, the better I play. However, you have to accept sometimes that you're not going to see enough ball in the right parts of the field, and that's the way it goes. You also have to accept that winning the game is more important than any one person's performance. On the other hand, I knew in my own mind that if I wanted to claim a test place three weeks ahead I was due a big game sooner rather than later.

We all set our own standards in rugby. All I can tell you about mine is that what really excites me is the fact that I've never played the perfect game, or even come close. I don't know what it is, and anyway

I don't think it's achievable. But you get these tantalizing glimpses and, if they were all to come together, then maybe, just maybe . . .

For some of the guys there wasn't even the glimpse because on this, as on every tour, there were casualties. The first player to make the lonely trip home was Paul Grayson. Having struggled with a groin injury all season it flared up again when we were at Weybridge, but 'Grays' decided to soldier on. None of us blamed him because we all knew that the opportunity to become a Lion does not come along very often but, having aggravated the injury playing against Border, he came to the end of the road after the Western Province match.

Professional or amateur, attitudes to injury don't vary – you always think, 'There, but for the grace of God, go I,' and with Paul it was no different. At the Sunday morning press conference Fran Cotton announced that Grays was on his way home and that the Lions management had faxed the England squad in Argentina requesting that Mike Catt – who had scored 21 points in their 46–20 first test victory over the Pumas – be allowed to join the tour. I was looking forward to reminding 'Catty' of my clairvoyant qualities. Fran, however, gave everybody a cold shower with his statistical revelation that, on average, six players on every Lions tour are forced to return home injured. That set us wondering just whose names would be written on the five remaining tickets.

After a 'recovery' session in the pool at the Institute of Sport at Newlands, we were whisked off to the airport for the flight to

Johannesburg, from where there was a 45-minute bus ride north to Pretoria, our home for the next ten days. When we got to Cape Town airport we discovered that there was a 'missing link' in the tour party. Johno had been left behind. He turned up in regal fashion soon afterwards in a chauffeur-driven BMW courtesy of the hotel.

No sooner had we got to the Pretoria Holiday Inn Crowne Plaza than Jason and myself took Grays along the road to Oscar's, a seedy chrome and plastic late-night bar 50 metres down the road from the hotel, for a farewell beer or two. We met the Sky TV crew in there, including my old Bath sparring partner Stuart 'Barrel' Barnes, and they did the honours as we wished Grays well on his road to recovery.

Pretoria is not only the administrative and political capital of South Africa, it is the place where you have the greatest sense of things being part of an alien culture. Pretoria and Cape Town are chalk and cheese. One of the main differences is that Afrikaans is the main language in Pretoria, and you hear much less English spoken. Consequently, even though it was probably subconscious, we withdrew into ourselves a bit more. It was us against the outside world.

That said, the South African press reaction to our victory over Western Province told us that we had done what Geech had asked us to: namely, to sow the seeds of doubt in the minds of the Springbok selectors and their players. The dismissive reaction from the first two games had been replaced by alarm bells – 'Lions sound a warning' and 'These Lions are no easy meat' were typical headlines – and Gavin

Rich, the rugby correspondent of the *Argus* chain of newspapers, captured the mood with the opening paragraph of his match report: 'They said that the Lions had forwards that were soft and were fatally deficient. We now know that is a load of garbage.'

How on earth the press manage to remain credible when they are prone to such amazing mood swings in the space of a few days is beyond me. It may not have been in quite the same league in terms of sensationalism as 'Freddie Star Ate My Hamster!', but we'd been transformed from pussycats to man-eaters in the space of three days.

Carel du Plessis, the new Springbok coach, was also in compliment-ary mood. 'They were very impressive,' said du Plessis. 'I was particu-larly impressed with their ball retention and the way they managed to round off.' Already du Plessis was being offered plenty of advice on how South Africa should handle the Lions, not least from Western Province's Viljoen. 'We're going to have to try and take them up-front, trying anything else might be suicidal,' said Viljoen. 'All my backline players spoke highly of the Lions backs, including James Small. I don't think we can beat the Lions by spreading the ball, because I think they have our number at the back.'

I didn't find these feast or famine assessments particularly convin-cing, but the one area we all knew was going to have to improve for us to stand an earthly in the test series was the scrummaging. Johno had put his finger on the pulse when he said, 'Province scrummaged tremendously well as a team, while we scrummaged as individuals – and it's something we will have to work on.'

At that stage Johno was blissfully unaware of just what amount of blood, sweat and tears were going to go into that work. Jim Telfer was not. 'British teams tend to go down and then relax before the ball comes in, while the South Africans maintain the intensity after the hit,' explained Telfer when we reached Pretoria. 'That is something we warned the players about beforehand, but there is nothing like first-hand experience to drum the message home,' he added ominously.

Although Pretoria is not the most 'happening' of places, there was plenty happening with us when it came to the training field. Simply put, Telfer went into 'beasting' overdrive. The main compensation was that most of us were pleased to be able to unpack and bed down in one spot for a while, rather than up sticks every couple of days. There might not have been a great deal going on in recreational terms – a bit of golf, go-karting and cinema – but there was time to rest up, and that was something most of us were happy enough doing. Particularly the forwards.

Jim began drumming home his message on Monday morning after the team for the Mpumalanga match had been selected, with Gregor Townsend and myself among the six on the bench. He gave the forwards a right seeing to. Scrummaging, mauling, the works. They even went back for a lineout session in the afternoon, which made us late for the Scottish Provident cocktail party that evening. Afterwards he described the way he had worked the eight due to play Mpumalanga on the Wednesday as 'the hardest I've worked forwards on a machine'. That was some admission from a 'beast artiste' like Telfer. They put down 46 scrums. That, as Andy Keast had pointed out prior to the tour, was virtually unheard of in terms of England training in recent years. It even meant something to me.

The machine – trademarked 'Predator' – was operated by the former England lock Nigel Horton, who was a partner in the firm that produced them. It was a monstrous lump of metal that looked like some instrument of torture from the Spanish Inquisition mounted on massive pitch rollers. Apparently it had the ability, through hydraulics, not only to measure the amount of shove, but also to push back against the poor sods trying to shift it. I occasionally offered up a silent prayer of thanks that I wasn't one of them. Horton became a bit like the spectre at the feast as he drove the length and breadth of South Africa – on one occasion in the black of night in the Transkei having to skirt around a dead body lying in the road – with the 'Predator' lurching around on the trailer behind his vehicle, ready and waiting once again to take the Lions forwards to hell and back.

From where I stood – which was as far away as possible – the bloody thing used to hiss and twitch, almost as if it was alive, as the forwards disengaged from one scrum before doing battle with it

again, while Telfer barked, cajoled, chided and downright slagged off anyone who showed any sign of flagging. By this time Jim seemed to have singled out Dai Young ('Ted') for special attention on a regular basis. It was like watching an army drill sergeant at work. It went something like this: 'David, get over here!', 'David, get over there!', 'David, pick up a bag and stand there!', 'David, get out the road!'

By comparison with what the forwards went through, the backs' sessions with Geech might have seemed a bit tame – but then so would getting into a swimming pool with a 15-foot croc that hadn't fed for a while. In fact, they were demanding and were made more so because the soreness and bruising from Saturday's match hadn't worn off. We did 10 against 10 contact exercises, in three teams. You worked flat out in either attack or defence for three minutes before your turn came to swap with the team that had been sitting it out, which meant that sometimes you would go straight from defence to attack before you got a breather, i.e. six minutes of continuous movement and contact. Repeat ad infinitum.

That night I had intended to go out, but I didn't have the energy. I stayed in and watched TV. I know I wasn't the only one.

Unbelievable. On Tuesday we were given the day off. Obviously Geech and the other Scottish 'Braveheart' had relented and we lost no time in getting a group together for a day's golf at a club 50 km out of town. Jase, Lol, Austin Healey, Tony Underwood, 'Babs' Regan, Dave

McLean and yours truly had a great day out, and our hosts couldn't do enough for us. The match went down to the last hole and finished all square.

In the evening back at the hotel the team for Mpumalanga went through the same drill as we had before the Western Province match, talking through the back-row moves and the lineout calls. I also caught up with some of the press-conference gossip where Jim Telfer had been asked for chapter and verse on yesterday's training session and had responded in true 'an hour spent not rucking is an hour wasted' fashion.

Asked whether his slagging off of players had ever backfired, Jim retorted, 'Aye, it's all done with a purpose, but no, I've never had a player say, "Don't say that tae me", and if they did, I'd say, "See my lawyer".'

As for the severity of the session, Jim conceded, 'It was quite tough, but they've got money in the bank now.' But he made no apologies – in fact, quite the opposite, as he outlined his method: 'I had a chat to the forwards yesterday and I told them that I see only two kinds of rugby players – the honest ones and the others. I told them that we were looking for players who don't look for excuses but get on and do something about it. Yesterday was about character, about getting into the guts of the session. The modern game is about playing with fatigue and pushing your body when it doesn't want to respond.'

His parting shot to the press on the scrummaging front was

'There's eight of them left, and they'll all be on the machine tomorrow.'
I thought, 'Sweet dreams, boys,' and decided to refer to myself as
'Honest' Jerry Guscott from then on.

Wednesday, 4 June: British Isles v. Mpumalanga

The South Africans announced their team for their warm-up game
against Tonga yesterday and the big, but not unsurprising news, was
that Gauteng's two 1995 World Cup stars, Kobus Wiese, a bruiser of
a lock, and Hennie Le Roux, a talented centre/fly-half, who had
played against us as 'guests' in the Eastern Province opener, had been
dropped. Carel du Plessis denied that their exclusion had anything to
do with their wage dispute with Louis Luyt, president of Gauteng as
well as SARFU. Seeing how both of them had played out of their
skins in the extended tour of Argentina, France and Wales six months
earlier, it left both Allan Bateman – who had played against them in
Cardiff – and myself sceptical that they had been left out on form
alone as we sat next to each other on the bus heading for Mpumalanga.

It wasn't the only topic of conversation. We also mulled over the
differences between the Welsh and English set-ups. Despite the fact
that we were competing against each other for the same test position
– Allan had recovered from a hamstring injury sustained against
Border and was playing against Mpumalanga – we had a pretty relaxed

relationship. It had a lot to do with the fact that we had both achieved a fair amount, had been around, were the same age, and didn't feel we had a lot to prove to each other. However, I reckon if he'd been playing as well he did on tour but was in his early twenties, there would have been calls early on for the old man, i.e. me, to move over. Obviously he wanted the test spot as much as I did, but when you've got a bit of experience under your belt you tend to be able to roll with the punches. It's easier at our age.

My outlook was straightforward, and I suspect 'Batman's' was similar. I'm not one for deep, meaningful analysis. My main yardstick is that I know that if I'm playing well I'm going to be close to selection for the main game, so you go out to do yourself justice. I also try to look at competition from other players as a positive rather than a negative. It motivates me when I see another player in my position playing well – and throughout the tour Allan kept me motivated.

The same couldn't be said for Alan Tait, mainly because he spent so much time away from the training grind because of what became a tour-long spate of niggling injuries. I doubt that he ever completed a full week's training because of one thing or another – he even blamed it on his age! - and, basically, he got away lightly. My feeling was that he should have been told to get out there like the rest of us. But Taity's a wise old bird, and the management seemed to be prepared to make an exception. He was helped by the fact that James Robson, the tour Doc, always erred on the side of caution with injuries, prescribing anything from two to four days' rest. Only thing was, Taity had always recovered by the time selection for the big games came along.

The drive out to Witbank, a big mining town in what used to be South East Transvaal, took a good two hours. We were expecting Mpumalanga to give us a hard game because they had not only thrashed Wales and then made the semi-finals of the previous year's Currie Cup, they were also meant to have a huge pack. I took my seat on the bench and waited for the monsters to make their entrance. When they did, I remember thinking, well, the ball boys have come out, but where are the rest of them? They were every bit an average-sized outfit. Then again, with blokes like Elandre van den Bergh in the side – the same bloke whose boots had left Jon Callard needing 27 stitches in his face after England's encounter with Eastern Province three years previously – perhaps they meant monsters of a different sort. Given what went on during the course of the afternoon, the term was appropriate enough.

The game was notable on two counts, one good and one as bad as it gets. The good news was that the Lions, one and all, took Mpumalanga to the cleaners, running in 10 tries. In the process Neil Back produced one of the best openside flanker displays I've ever seen.

The bad was the career-threatening knee-ligament injury sustained by Doddie Weir early in the second half thanks to his opposite number, Marius Bosman, who came round the side of a ruck to deliver a karate-style downward kick to Weir's outstretched leg. Doddie had been cleaning Bosman out at the lineout, and both he and van den Bergh – who seemed intent on proving that a leopard never changes his spots – had already started putting in sly punches and trampling anything in a red shirt. Video analysis by the management team put their extra-curricular activities in double figures.

Bosman wasn't fit to lace Weir's boots as a player, and what he did was plain disgusting. At the time I spent a lot of the game following the ball rather than looking at the off the ball incidents, but the next day watching the video was 'Hammer Horror' stuff. You saw the incident once and turned away – you didn't want to see it again. I couldn't believe what I was watching. I almost had to do a double-take to make sure that the guy had on a rugby shirt, shorts and boots and that it wasn't a brawl in the street. Bosman deserved an absolute slating. Only a weak man can make an attack like that. It was such a cheap shot, so callous, so unnecessary. In the process he wilfully jeopardized another professional sportsman's career and put a man's livelihood at risk. Initially I would have been happy to see him banned for a year, and thought the minimum he would get would be six months. But as the extent of the injury became clear I became of the Old Testament 'eye-for-an-eye' view that, if it ended Doddie's career, there was no reason why it shouldn't also end Bosman's.

I find the lack of consistency in the way that rugby administrators deal with on-field violence hard to credit. It's worrying. If a common assault like that of Bosman on Weir had happened outside the rugby pitch you could be looking at a prison sentence – and, in this country, as Gloucester's Simon Devereux discovered when he was sent to prison, civil proceedings can be brought for assault on the pitch too. However, what's weird is when a bloke like Neil Back can be banned in England for six months for a little shove on a referee, while someone like Bosman can walk away pretty well unscathed.

Despite Fran Cotton's furious reaction, Bosman was allowed to get off on a technicality by SARFU. The tour agreement between the Four Home Unions and our hosts specified – ridiculously in my view – that, if there was an incident on the field that the referee ruled on there and then, the perpetrator basically could not be cited after the event. In other words, even if the culprit had jumped up and down on someone's head until they were unconscious, if the referee took action there and then there would be no secondary trial by video. Ludicrous.

The only means, therefore, for Bosman to be punished was if the Mpumalanga union took action against their own player. When they eventually did, it left Doddie, his mother Nan, who had called for Bosman to be suspended for a season, and Fran and Geech spitting blood. Bosman was fined 10,000 Rand, which is about £1400. And that, folks, was that. No ban, nothing.

Willem Strauss, the Mpumalanga chief executive, explained that 'Marius will definitely be paying the fine . . . and this money will be redistributed for the development of rugby in our province . . . seeing this is a professional era, we decided to hit him where it hurts most, in his pocket.' He added that Bosman was a part-time player who didn't have a huge contract: 'As a fitter-and-turner, Marius isn't well paid, so he will be paying this fine over the next three months or so.' Perhaps he wouldn't have had that minor inconvenience if the Mpumalanga officials had taken their responsibilities seriously enough not to have selected him in the first place.

Meanwhile, Doddie, out of the tour, career in the balance, surgery to come, was left to contemplate taking out a civil action against Bosman if he wanted to get any sort of justice. If it had been my knee, I would have gone after him in the courts. Part of the game plan in South Africa seems to be to treat violent players with a sort of world-weary 'boys will be boys' shrug and shake of the head. The South Africans are not honest, open or hard enough on themselves when it comes to discipline. The Bosman affair was not a great statement for their game. The sooner that sort of incident is wiped from its face, the more people will respect them.

As a squad we were furious with the way in which the whole incident was handled by the South Africans but, as Fran Cotton said, we had made the best representations we could and, unfortunately, the ball was now in Doddie's court. I told Doddie, who had been playing well, how sorry I was that his tour had had to end in that way, wished him luck with the operation, and told him I looked forward to seeing him turning out for Newcastle early next season at Bath. But, as Fran said, we now had to put the incident behind us and move on.

At least Mpumalanga got their just deserts on the pitch. They came unstuck by trying to bulldoze their way through our pack, in which the front row of 'Wally' (Richard Wallace), 'Woody' (Keith Wood) and 'The Boston Strangler' (Tom Smith) made a strong impression, and then we skinned them with some good continuity. Rob Wainwright, who had been replaced as captain by Tim Rodber, came back with a bang by getting the ball rolling with a hat-trick of tries in the first 20 minutes.

I was on my toes because Ieuan Evans had a bit of a calf strain a couple of days prior to the match and was winding me up by saying he wasn't sure whether it would hold out. So, during the game, I gave him a bit of stick saying what a chicken, gutless git and weed he'd be if he even contemplated coming off. It worked a treat. Ieuan played the whole match and, I reckon, had me to thank for the two-try flourish with which he rounded off a fine team performance.

However, the day did not finish with the final whistle. The team bus was soon belting its way back to Pretoria ready for those who had not played to be put through their paces on one of the floodlit training pitches at the impressive Loftus Versfeld stadium, the venue for Saturday's game against Northern Transvaal. The 'Predator' was lying in wait.

There was nothing self-congratulatory about this session. Despite the margin of victory Geech was not ready to let any complacency creep in. While he yelled at us backs, 'We dropped the sodding ball 10 times in the last 10 minutes', Jim was about to pick up where he'd left off. The eight to play Northern Transvaal were going to get a gutful – but none of them were saying, 'For what we are about to receive, will the Lord make us truly thankful.'

As the steam rose from the scrum and the machine hissed, all I could hear, apart from the collective grunts and groans as they engaged the metal nightmare, was the voices of Jim Telfer and Ronnie Regan. Ronnie sounded demented. If there's such a thing as a West Country banshee, it had possessed him. Every time he and the rest of the eight disengaged, Telfer would send them loping around the posts with a few choice words like 'We'd have been pushed back five yards – do it again.' Consequently, when they returned to do battle with the beast, Ronnie would glare at it before unleashing a blood-curdling scream: 'Yew *-!-#-@-E-R!' howled Ronnie as the front row went for the hit. Forty-five times Ronnie howled. On occasions, however, another sound broke through like rolling thunder. A half-expectant, half-ecstatic bellow which carried to the four corners of the pitch and probably half of Pretoria beyond as it reverberated around the empty stands of the stadium: 'Hold the world, boys! Hold the world!'

It was Jim – and Jim was in his element.

Chapter 6

GORED BY THE BLUE BULLS

It was great to see Catty on tour, particularly as we were entering the part of the itinerary which Fran Cotton had dubbed the 'Bermuda Triangle', namely the three games in seven days against the strongest provincial sides in the country, the Super 12 trio of Northern Transvaal, Gauteng and Natal. We all knew it was a tall order and I was delighted we had a player of Catty's calibre to call on. Fran had picked him up from the airport and driven him straight to the Mpumalanga game, after which we trained together at Loftus. I told Mike that, seeing as I'd predicted before we left the UK that he would end up with the Lions, old 'Madame Vasso' was way off the pace compared to me.

The most likely reason why Mike wasn't selected in the first place was that the Lions selectors thought he was too much of a risk. I would have picked him simply because I've played with him so much. He also happens to be one of the most talented backs I've come across in northern-hemisphere rugby, and he showed as much last season against Wales. Given the right ball he can more than dictate a game from fly-half.

After the match, it was again the desert after the oasis as the South Africans reverted to giving us very little credit for what we'd achieved. Yes, the Lions had won – but Mpumalanga were useless. Then the old cat-call came out: 'Wait until we get you here, wait until we get you there . . .'

What they failed to realize was that we were our own harshest critics. Nobody was more aware than the Lions that if we'd stayed with our game plan we would have beaten Mpumalanga by 20–30 points more. But because we opened it up, loosened up and made some silly mistakes, they were able to capitalize on some of them. That said, it's human nature that when something is easier than expected you are not as demanding of yourself as you would be if it was fiercely competitive.

The team to play Northerns, otherwise known as the 'Blue Bulls', was announced on Thursday and I was on the bench for the second match running – and I didn't know why. Catty was also on the bench so perhaps Geech wanted someone around him with whom he was familiar. Then during morning training 'Batman' pulled out due to injury and, Bob's your uncle, I was in the starting line-up. I took the rest of the day as a rest day. While the non-playing squad had the delight of a reception at the British Consulate, I went to the cinema and saw Jim Carrey in *Liar, Liar*, which was probably a good deal more fun.

Much as I enjoyed it, when I got back to the hotel I felt a bit low. It was probably a combination of mid-term tour blues and not quite knowing where the selection policy or game plan was going, so I sought out Geech and had a chat with him about training and what we were aiming to achieve, particularly where 'Igor' Townsend and the forwards were concerned.

I told Geech that I felt the backs needed to be more physical in our training, that we should wear the bodysuits and go full out as we had early in the tour – i.e. that it should mirror match conditions as closely as possible. I was worried also that we were beginning to play a forward-style game to which we weren't best suited. Jim had been urging the forwards to pick up and drive, pick up and drive, go through the same hole, keep tight and ram through the middle of the opposition. It seemed to me that the drawback was that they were getting tied up in the loose and all the backs were getting was very slow ball with which it was virtually impossible to create anything and launch a decent attack. To me, quick ball was the key to the running game we wanted to play.

The other concern was Igor's concentration span. I was aware that I couldn't have a go at him all the time because it might get to him so much that it totally messed up his game. My reasoning was that Geech, who worked with him all the time at Northampton, was in a far better position to give him a gentle kick up the backside and tell him to start working and concentrating.

Personally I was very relaxed on the trip regarding my own form. The only time I was a little bit miffed was, in this instance, finding myself on the bench a couple of times in a row. Initially I put it down to the coaches wanting to have a look at all the various combinations in the centre. The only problem as far as the original selection for the Northerns game was that I couldn't see the pairing of Allan Bateman and Alan Tait as a combination. On the '93 tour I went for 10 days without a game – which had it not been for injuries would have happened in South Africa as well – and that would have meant I needed to put in a big game in midweek just to say I'm still here and still playing well. What put me out of kilter on this tour was the way that the management delayed selection right up to the last minute to cater for those with niggling injuries. Most players want as much time as possible to prepare mentally for a game, and I'm no different.

So, I had a lot on my mind, and I had to get it off. Geech said he knew where I was coming from, would take it into account and that we should move on. I felt better for having clarified things and was also delighted to hear that another of my Bath team-mates on the England tour of Argentina, Ollie Redman, was being flown over as a replacement for Doddie Weir and was due to arrive in 24 hours.

Any criticism of my team-mates, such as Gregor, related to the frustrations you get within any human enterprise. It doesn't necessarily mean that you're at each other's throats, and Gregor and I got on fine. Overall one of the great strengths of this Lions party was the mutual respect there was among us. Tom Smith, for instance, was one of the quietest men many of us had ever come across – he seemed to speak only when he wanted something, and that was rare – but nobody was phased by it and Tom was a popular tourist. There were no rifts along national lines as had happened in '93 with the Scottish dirt trackers – we were, as Geech had emphasized throughout, Lions first and foremost. That's not to say people didn't favour particular groups – Dai Young and Scott Gibbs are close friends, as I am with Jason Leonard and Lawrence Dallaglio – but at no stage would I ever walk into the team room or the dinner room and think, 'I'm not sitting next to him or them.' I knew that a bloke like Ollie, the veteran's veteran, would only add to the 'all for one, one for all' attitude that ran through the Lions squad.

The other thing that was on my mind was that Jayne was fast approaching the delivery date for our third baby. I phoned her every day, sometimes twice, just to have a chat and check that everything was all right. As soon as we knew she was pregnant right at the start of the season we had discussed the Lions tour with the awareness that, if I went, I would be away when the baby was born. Obviously it was something we had to discuss and resolve, and while Jayne didn't exactly jump up and down for joy, she knew that it was important to me, and I went with her blessing. But no, there were no romantic candle-lit dinners with me begging her on bended knee to let me go, and she saying, 'Yes, Dwarling, you must go.'

It never occurred to me when she was due to go into labour that I might go to Fran Cotton and ask him whether I could fly home for the birth, stay a day and then fly back – he might even have said yes. But I never asked because I didn't think it was feasible on a Lions tour. It was a big disappointment not to be there, but it was a decision Jayne and I had talked about and come to terms with.

Friday started with a light training session, which went well. Everyone seemed to be clicking and there was a sense of optimism as we shaped up for our biggest challenge of the tour so far. Afterwards I had a massage from Richard Wegrzyk, 'The Painless Pole', who is also an acupuncturist. He stuck some needles in me and I drifted off for about half an hour and woke up feeling totally refreshed.

I went downstairs, woozy and relaxed and I glided across the lobby in the direction of the team room. Half-way across the polished marble floor I got a hell of a shock. What should I see but one of the most highly polished bald domes in rugby emerging from the back seat of a car. Even though I'd known that Ollie was due to arrive, it was a real jolt actually seeing him in the flesh. It took that much to make it register that he had actually become a British Lion. I went down to greet him but couldn't help myself. The first words that came out were 'What are you doing here?' 'I'm not sure,' said Ollie. It didn't take any of us long to find out.

Nigel 'Ollie' Redman is one of Bath's great unsung heroes, and after a decade of sterling service, which has included winning 19 England caps on and off since 1985, last season he decided to phase himself out gradually from playing into coaching. However, when locks started getting a bit thin on the ground for the tour of Argentina who did Jack Rowell call on to dig him out of a hole but one of his trusty old servants.

When Fran Cotton delivered the double whammy of requesting that Catt and Redman make the hop across the Atlantic to join the Lions in the week between England's two tests against the Pumas, happy and Jack were not words that went together according to Ollie. But, as there often was among the Bath 'family', a sense of mickey-taking humour was never far away.

'Jack Rowell called me into his hotel room in Argentina and told me they wanted me for South Africa. I told Jack that I couldn't believe it.

"Neither can I," said Jack.'

The story has already become part of rugby folklore and, certainly at Bath, so has Ollie. That evening, sat around the dinner table in the Holiday Inn with myself and some of the press, he demonstrated why by recounting tales of his life and times as one of England's most dropped locks, the ever handy 'fall guy'. Ollie has the gift of being able to laugh at himself which, given some of the stories, is just as well.

The one that stood out was how, after a superb performance in England's 1993 victory over New Zealand at Twickenham, having been hailed as the man of the match, he had not unreasonably expected that he might keep his place in the side. At the next squad weekend he had arrived at the hotel in Richmond when, after a short while, the England manager, Geoff Cooke, had come over and told him that he had been dropped, this time in favour of Martin Bayfield.

Ollie recalled it like this: '"What do I do now?" I said to Geoff. He told me that if I hurried I could reach the hotel up the hill where the A team were staying, and catch the bus they were taking to their training session. I didn't have a car so I had to run up the road carrying my bags.

'As I lurched down the driveway with bags hanging off me left, right and centre, I realized that I was running right past the windows of the room where the England team, with all the blokes I'd played alongside a few days before, were holding a meeting. They were all watching.'

He had us in stitches. Which is quite appropriate really, because he's one of the most accident-prone people on the face of the earth. Once, during a warm-up in the changing rooms at Bath, with the studs ringing on the floor, he caught his foot in a bucket, crashed to the floor, and in the process cut that famous bald cranium.

It was great to have him on our side.

Saturday, 7 June: British Isles v. Northern Transvaal

This was the one that got away. We knew it was going to be hard, but we made it harder for ourselves.

The day didn't dawn too well for me because I didn't get a good night's sleep thanks to 'Snake's' (Scott Gibbs) snoring. I had breakfast with Ian McGeechan and we mulled over our respective international futures and various other rugby matters during which he revealed that he had just signed a new six-year contract with Northampton. The morning newspaper, the Pretoria News, carried a huge colour cartoon on the front page showing three petrified-looking Lions (animal type) trapped in the Loftus arena staring down the barrels of a thousand rifles. No prizes for guessing we're in the heartland of Afrikanerdom.

The backs had a meeting at 11 a.m. and the confidence from the training was still evident. On our arrival at the ground, a small group of chanting Lions supporters greeted the bus, but they were going to have difficulty making themselves heard in this impressive stadium.

It all went belly up in the first 30 minutes. We came out of the blocks very slowly and it felt flatter than at any stage on tour. Nobody seemed to be willing to take a lead. It was like playing with strangers. Weird, a strange atmosphere. Even stranger considering that the build-up in the changing room had been purposeful, we'd come off a good midweek win, the pitch was in great condition and the opposition were shorn of their five Springboks and, apart from a draw with the eventual winners, Auckland, had had an average Super 12. So why did we freeze?

Perhaps it had something to do with the 'Pink Salmon'. Fran, I heard later, had been interviewed on the pitch prior to the match over the p.a. system and had tempted fate by saying that, despite the traditional strength of the Blue Bulls, in his own career he had never been on a losing side at Loftus. Perhaps it had something to do with the 'Bermuda Triangle', because we certainly got lost somewhere. Seriously though, nobody could put their finger on what went wrong.

We were 11–0 down after 22 minutes and, frankly, we were lucky that it wasn't more. They were all over us up front, in both tight and loose phases, and a couple of penalties either side of a try by their goal-kicking left wing, Casper Steyn, left us in no doubt that Northerns were a side with strength in depth. Their backs ran hard and straight and regrouped quickly to outnumber us when they got quick possession.

We had to get ourselves into the game. In training we had been working off the principle that the numbers on our backs were purely there for first-phase play, and that once that was over they became irrelevant. Consequently, when the ball came to me in the fly-half position in broken play after 24 minutes I sensed that the Northerns' backs had been caught flat and there was a gap to exploit. This was a South African defensive frailty that Andy Keast, our technical assistant, had pinpointed and it had been suggested that we use either chip kicks or grubbers to exploit it. I would have liked to have run through the gap, but when it closed quickly I decided immediately to chip and follow up. When their full back, Graeme Bouwer, failed to snaffle it I managed to keep my balance in the contact, toe the ball on, and then gather it just before the line to dive over.

It was a satisfying moment, and I was pleased to have got away with it, but it didn't turn the match around. Frustration was building up, we were starting to niggle at the referee and conceded 10 metres twice, we were having to play catch-up rugby and, because of the quality of the opposition, there was a good deal of tension. A try by van Schalkwyk, their Springbok centre, made the half-time score 18–7. When their no. 8 and captain, Adriaan Richter, scored from a back-row move off the back of a scrum just one minute into the second half, at 25–7 it looked like 'Goodnight, Irene.'

Then, courtesy of Gregor's dummy and neat inside pass, I managed to cut through and score under the posts, and a Tim Stimpson conversion and two penalties later the deficit was a mere 25–20 and the revival was in full swing with the Lions forwards coming on to their game approaching the final quarter. The match was in the balance, but disaster was lurking round the corner in the form of a suicidal pass from Gregor which was picked off by van Schalkwyk, who ran clear for his second try of the afternoon. It was enough to make you weep and, although Gregor got on the score sheet with a try five minutes from time, the bubble had already burst.

One of the main differences between Northerns and the other sides we had played was that this time we were punished for the mistakes that we made. The biggest one was obviously Gregor's interception gift early in the second half. We were not good on this tour at putting in those 50-metre clearances that relieve the pressure at critical times and, to be fair to Northerns, they turned the screw effectively.

It seemed that every time we tried to clear our lines, somehow the ball always ended up slicing off the outside of someone's boot. It was a pity because we were more than capable of winning it. But I'm not prepared to make excuses because they took their chances and we made the mistakes.

Normally it takes a side five minutes to get a shaky start out of its system. Someone does something inspirational and you're on your way. With the Lions that afternoon nothing, bar that first try, worked for the first half hour. Mind you, Bentos had quite an effect on Steyn.

Early in the game I heard someone yelling at me from the right-hand touchline. It was Bentos. 'Hey, Jerry, look at him! Look at him!' I wondered what the hell he was on about. I said 'Look at what?'

Bentos bellowed back: 'Look at my bloody winger. I'm going to @#!*'@! terrorize him.' He made such a ferocious din that there was no way that Steyn could have mistaken his intentions. Fear had a wonderfully galvanizing effect on the 23-year-old Blue Bulls winger. He finished the game with a personal haul of 20 points, including a try, three conversions and three penalties – and Bentos hardly laid a hand on him.

After the match, John Williams, the Northerns' and former Springbok coach, who the hacks say ignores any questions that are not preceded by his academic title of Professor, said that the Lions would have to learn a few lessons if we wanted to compete successfully with southern-hemisphere sides. They don't stand on ceremony the South Africans – win a game, and the teach-in is never far away.

'The one thing the Lions have got to realize is that if they want to play this type of game, they've got to start scrumming and driving – you must tie your opponent in with driving play.' He also conceded, 'They're a very good team, and if you let them run with the ball you are heading for trouble.'

As I've said before, I'm no scrummaging expert, but there's no doubt that in the early Saturday games we were under the cosh in that department where the midweek pack, particularly Smith, Wood and Wallace against Mpumalanga, didn't seem to be.

The other main fall-out from the game involved the two Welsh Scotts, Gibbs and Quinnell. Snake, who had come on for Bentos in the final quarter for his first run since turning his ankle against Border, had been cited by Northerns for a punch thrown when he tackled winger Grant Esterhuizen. Meanwhile Scotty Quinnell sustained a groin strain serious enough to end his tour. He was the third player to have to head home and, given his strengths on the ball, it was a great shame. However, by that stage we were all becoming pretty philosophical about injuries – we had to be.

A philosophical outlook helped where that evening's dinner was concerned. Just when we needed a lift, needed to book a restaurant with a bit of ambience to take us out of ourselves, all the Chardonnay Kid had managed to find was another packed-out O'Hagan's. On the way back from the meal most of the lads got out of the bus at Hatfield, a typical South African mall-village full of bars and restaurants, where they went to a bar called the Sports Frog. The only difficulty with places like Hatfield is the strange sense that it's all been built around a fortress mentality. You're eating and drinking in a kind of food, beverage and shopping fortress where all the different interests have been thrown together, first and foremost, for security reasons.

I went back to the hotel where, having received various pats on the back for my two tries and one 'assist', I got stuck into a few bottles of red wine courtesy of the media. From there it was on to Oscar's to bid farewell to Scott Quinnell. It was a big night on the grog, and I, among others, ended up getting wrecked.

*

The following day Scottish Provident, our main tour sponsors, had organized a golf day for us, them, their clients and the British and South African media. I had intended to make it, but sometimes the best-laid plans of mice and men . . .

Suffering badly, I spent most of the day in bed, and then raised enough energy to get up and go and lounge around the hotel until dinner. That evening we had a team meeting at 8 where, surprise, surprise, we concluded that we had made too many mistakes. After the post-mortem I made another one. I decided that I required another beer and joined Snake, Scotty, Batman, Jase, the Doc and Carcass (physio Mark Davies) in Oscar's.

That morning Snake had had to attend a disciplinary meeting with Fran to answer the citing, which had apparently been initiated at the insistence of the Northerns' players. According to one of them, their reasoning was: 'If one of our guys had done this overseas he would have had the book thrown at him.' It was presided over by a real judge, a Judge Daniels, and the minutes of the meeting were suitably grave and, although I don't condone the punch, frankly, a bit of a laugh.

'Mr Gibbs indicated that he pleaded not guilty . . . and explained that, "He was attempting to dislodge the ball where it was held by Esterhuizen under his arm."

'It is our unanimous decision that Mr Gibbs threw a deliberate punch. The explanation offered by Mr Gibbs appears to us to be rather fanciful regard being had to . . . the clear impression that he deliberately cocked his right arm before delivering the punch. We have taken into account the fact that no injury resulted, since the blow was glancing. We understand that Mr Gibbs is a former League player, and that he is accustomed to playing the game maybe more aggressively. That may be so, but he should adapt his game to comply with the rules adopted by the International Board.'

The upshot was that 'Mr Gibbs' was given a one-match ban, which put him out of the reckoning for the make-or-break game of the 'Bermuda Triangle' against Gauteng in midweek. It was almost worth it for the humour the minutes provided.

The full implications of Snake's ban hit home, however, when I was selected for the bench for the third time on the trot – which meant that I would probably end up playing because Allan Bateman, who had been paired with 'Shaggy' Greenwood, had still got a hamstring problem. I wasn't best pleased, particularly as Alan Tait seemed to have acquired yet another injury, which would no doubt keep him out just until the weekend.

I went to training with a bad hangover and things didn't improve when I got a cut above the eye. This brought an abrupt halt to my session but made me fair game for the tour jokers, who wasted no time in getting on my case. I heard 'Who's a pretty boy, then?' so many times I began to think I was the tour parrot. I felt pretty bushed and, although in this instance some of it was self-inflicted,

I had no qualms about taking myself off to bed for the afternoon.

While I was in my pit, some of the lads, including Lol (Lawrence Dellaglio), Richard Hill and Rob Howley, went to Soweto – where soccer, the game favoured by most black South Africans, is king – to take part in a development coaching clinic. One of the township schools represented there, Jubalani, had just clinched a sponsorship deal with Virgin Atlantic, the Lions' official carrier. Jubalani, appropriately enough, translates as 'Happiness'.

Although we had just suffered our first reverse, our self-belief was not shaken. As a squad our resolve was underpinned by the fact that we knew we had the fire-power to do well. That's not to say we weren't human and weren't capable of being thrown off beam by what was written and said about us, but in that respect being isolated in the heart of Afrikanerdom was no bad thing. We were able to feed off each other's determination – if you were down, there was always somebody else who was up – and there were a lot of very determined characters in the 1997 Lions.

Our mind-set was one of making sure that we learned from our mistakes and improved with every game we played. When you make that your yardstick, rather than purely the winning or the losing, you take a lot pressure off your shoulders. Our attitude at the time was that even if we lost to Gauteng just so long as we had improved on our performance against Northerns we were on the right track.

We accepted that two losses in a row would have seen us written off by the South African press, who had already started along that route, while the British press would have had a field day. Increasingly the attitude among us was 'So what?'

We were given another day off training on Tuesday so I surfaced late, had a chat to Keasty, Lol and Chris Jones of the *Evening Standard*, and then went down to the Health & Rackets club in mid-afternoon to work out. I discovered also that Tony Diprose, the Saracens no. 8 capped recently on the England tour of Argentina, had been called in as a replacement for Scott Quinnell. It came as a bit of a surprise that he had been given the nod ahead of my former Bath team-mate, Ben Clarke, who was also in Argentina. Clarkie's pedigree as a big-game player was unquestionable, and his form for the Lions in New Zealand in '93 was outstanding. However, since joining (the then) second-division Richmond last year, Clarkie's international career had taken even more of a nose-dive than mine – only he didn't have the opportunity of a Lions tour to put things right.

At the evening team meeting Ian McGeechan made an impassioned call for us to stick to the values of playing an open, running game and reiterated why we were committed to it. We go back a long way, Geech and I, and I agreed fundamentally with his drive to get British and Irish rugby at international level away from the 'comfort zone' of closing things down when the pressure is on. He encouraged us at every turn to break free of the shackles of safety-first rugby and play a flexible 15-man game.

That night I joined the card school and played until late. We could afford to because we were about to have our first evening kick-off of the tour and were due a lie-in the following morning. What we couldn't afford was the £350 that ended up in 'Shaggy' Greenwood's pocket at the close of play.

Chapter 7

SEEING OFF THE LESSER LIONS

Match day dawned, but I didn't dawn with it. Instead I got up at midday, had a late breakfast and went in search of 'The Painless Pole' in the hope of getting a rub down, only to discover that he had gone training with the remainder of the squad. I lounged around before phoning Jayne and talking to my second-born daughter, Holly, about the gym class she'd just been to.

When the boys returned from training, I was told that Batman's hamstring had not passed the fitness test and, as I'd suspected, Geech told me that I'd be playing my third game in 10 days. They say, however, that every cloud has a silver lining and things became a great deal brighter when Geech informed me that after the Gauteng game I could look forward to a 10-day rest. It was tantamount to telling me that I was already pencilled in for the first test. It was a real bonus – but I've been around long enough not to start counting my chickens. I didn't take it 100 per cent for granted that I was in the test side because, if I played badly against Gauteng and Batman played well on his next outing, I knew it would again be in the balance. I got that much-needed rub-down from 'Painless', and started to focus on the business in hand.

Tim Rodber was captaining the side, while Ollie Redman, proud as punch, was about to make his debut in the famous red jersey that he had never expected to pull on. It's hard to explain how it felt to have him playing in the same team, particularly as only a few weeks earlier I had seen him in Bath with a knee swollen like a balloon just after a major operation. I could still hear Andy Robinson's less than dulcet tones as he told the old warhorse, 'You'd better get used to coaching – because that's what you're going to be doing full-time next season.' Ollie's had so many injuries that I'm sure that when they put him under a scanner even the bloody machine tells him that it's time to pack in. Instead, what did he do? Had the knee op, went to Argentina a week after it, picked up another cap, and then found his way to South Africa. He had always been known for tremendous powers of recovery, but that was taking the mickey.

I knew, from years of playing together, that there was no one better to have up front in a game which the South African press had gleefully billed as 'Make or Break' for the Lions. Ollie was as solid as they come, and would be determined to make himself into the 'magnificent afterthought' they suggested he might become if he could handle 'the massive presence of Kobus Wiese'. With Catty also making his

Lions debut that evening, it was something of a Bath reunion. I wasn't complaining.

Wednesday, 11 June: British Isles v. Gauteng

Gauteng were expected to beat us – by everyone but us. They were Super 12 hardened, at full strength with the exception of Japie Mulder, the Springbok centre, and included Wiese, their captain, and Hennie Le Roux, who both had points to make to the South African selectors.

On the basis of what I'd seen in the Super 12, I thought it was going to be a very hard match. I had a picture of Ellis Park imprinted on my mind from watching a Super 12 final a couple of years before between Transvaal, as they were then, and Auckland. I remembered thinking just how much Auckland had to contend with. Massive crowd, massive game, massive opposition (then led by François Pienaar), not to mention massive pace and massive altitude.

As it turned out, one of the trademarks of the tour was the way we came strong in the final 20 minutes and South African sides were unable to live with us. Northerns had struggled to hold us in the final quarter and against Gauteng we went one better. Given everything we'd seen and all the southern-hemisphere crowing about how much faster the Super 12 was than anything the northern hemisphere had to offer, I couldn't believe how unfit some of their sides were,

Gauteng included. Either that, or our base fitness from our club game and the draconian training regime on tour had reaped dividends. In the last quarter we killed sides – they simply weren't in it. It was as if they gave up the ghost, they just stopped playing. Their forwards in particular were so physically exhausted they simply couldn't go on any more.

It was strange. I'd seen this Super 12 rugby on TV that seemed to be played at breakneck pace, whereas in reality it couldn't have been that quick or physically demanding if the Lions were wearing these sides down after 60 minutes. Perhaps we were super-fit. After all, we were playing them on their own turf, in an intimidating arena, at altitude we had barely had time to acclimatize to. Not only that, but Jo'burg is 1000 feet higher than Pretoria.

When you walk out of the tunnel on to the pitch at Ellis Park you are struck by the sheer size of the place – it and its surroundings seem more like a small town than a stadium. I had never played there before, and the only disappointment that evening was that the place wasn't full, because even half full (38,000) the atmosphere was crackling. Perhaps it has something to do with playing under lights. Catty and I went out to warm up and kicked a few spirals, and there were a few incomprehensible cat-calls (no pun intended) directed at us from the crowd in Afrikaans. It did cross my mind that, being black and one of only two players in the near vicinity, they might be directed at me, but it was equally likely they were shouting at Catty. Remember he was born in South Africa. Whatever, racist banter from crowds, or elsewhere, was not something that was rife in South Africa, in my experience, in the summer of '97. Times change, even at Ellis Park.

What doesn't change is the roar that greets the side with the distinctive single red-hooped jersey they now call the Gauteng Lions. They came at us full tilt for the first 15 minutes. In the initial bust-up I thought it was all going to be forward bashing, stomping, banging and bruising, but instead they spread the ball from side to side and really stretched us, playing totally committed 15-man rugby. It took me by surprise – and I made sure I wasn't the only one.

In the heat of the moment, when you've run and tackled about as much as you can and your eyeballs are out on stalks, there are occasional moments of pure farce, even at the top end of the game. At half-time we were annoyed with ourselves. We'd realized that we were committing too many forwards to the breakdown and leaving ourselves short of bodies out wide. No sooner had the second half kicked-off than I saw Paul Wallace heading for a ruck that looked as if it was already won. I yelled at him, 'Stay out, stay out! Get behind so you can come as a second wave!' The next second the ruck ball wasn't looking so promising, and I found myself roaring, 'Get stuck in! Get in there!' Wally looked like rugby's answer to *Riverdance*. He didn't know whether he was coming or going.

There was no denying that we had been up against it in the first half and, of the ball we got, we turned over far too much to put them under sustained pressure. Consequently, with Catty hitting the uprights twice with penalties for a tally of one from four attempts, we turned round at half-time 9 – 3 down, with Gauteng's points all coming from the boot of full back Dawie du Toit.

We were also having trouble relating to the decisions of Tappe Henning, who as South Africa's top referee had recently had control of the Super 12 final between Auckland and ACT (Australian Capital Territory). Geech and Fran had made it a policy that they would not be putting the boot into referees to explain our shortcomings. It was up to us to adapt to local conditions and we knew already, because it had crept into British refereeing as well, that both sides would be allowed to get away with putting the ball in crooked at the scrums and lineouts. Nevertheless, throughout the tour we had been dogged by the way the South Africans refereed the tackle and the breakdown. Basically they allowed anybody, whether they were on or off their feet, to secure possession. More than that, they seemed to be obsessed with the idea that the side taking the ball into the tackle should get it back (bar a knock-on), irrespective of whether the defending side had won it fair and square.

It seemed to be cast in tablets of stone where Henning was concerned. He proved the point on the half-hour when du Toit put Gauteng ahead 6 – 3 after Neil Back, who had a superb first half in defence, turned their lock Bruce Thorne in the tackle and the ball was ripped off him. A ruck was never formed, and the ball never touched the ground. It wasn't hard to understand why we were looking forward to neutral referees come the tests.

The Lions defence was watertight. One factor that was becoming obvious was that South African sides like Gauteng were so used to overpowering the opposition and getting their own way that when they came up against really stern resistance, they were stumped. You could almost see them wilt.

One of Ollie Redman's post-match anecdotes captured the Lions' mood at Ellis Park that evening. 'One of their props gave me a whack after I pulled Kobus Wiese down at a line-out. He said that if I did it again, then so would he. I blew him a kiss and told him that it was going to be a long night.' Kobus had a quiet game, while Ollie came through like an old trooper. Under the glare of the floodlights I even saw that shining dome, glinting with perspiration, looming up in support when I made a half-break. It was a reassuring sight.

Having soaked up their pressure we turned the tables on Gauteng in the second half. Initially, however, we were unable to make the breakthrough. Then, just past the hour, after a long drive by the pack up to their 22, a move featuring Bentos, Rodber, Williams and Greenwood gave Austin Healey – who had had mixed fortunes until then – a glimpse of their line. A little jink threw the full back, and 'Scally' scooted home. Neil Jenkins's touchline conversion gave us the lead, 10–9.

Four minutes later came the 'moment of all moments' – in John Bentley's eyes at least. Bentos got the ball 15 metres inside our half and, seeing they were lopsided in defence, started off on this run. He headed for the open space on the right wing. I knew he was going to get outside James Dalton, the Springbok hooker, so I went on the support run thinking, 'It's going to be an easy try for me, I've only got one or two men to beat after he gives me the inside pass.' I'm still waiting. Instead, he ran past me heading back towards the middle of the field. Not for the first time I thought, 'What the hell is he doing?' What he did was go on to score one of the great individual tries, leaving half the Gauteng side in his wake by first cutting across the grain of the cover defence and then straightening for the line. It encapsulated not only Bentley's spirit, but the spirit of the side as a whole. It was one of the defining moments of the tour.

With 'Jenko' converting and then hitting a 45-metre penalty from the touchline to give us a 20–9 lead, we should have buried them once and for all. Catty made a break and, when I cut inside with the line in my sights, he found me with a pass which, although a bit hard, I should have held.

Although they scored a consolation try in the last minute through flanker Andre Vos, when the final whistle blew we knew that, despite an unpromising start, we had kept our faith, toughed it out, and done the business. The satisfaction was immense. The tour was back on the road.

There was just one little postscript. While we were having dinner at the ground I suggested to Wally that, if ever he needed a choreographer, I was his man. We both cracked up.

Chapter 8

NETTING SHARKS IN NATAL

Having seen off the challenge from the lesser Lions, in the eyes of the South African media we again became serious contenders where the test series was concerned. The arrogance was something else. 'British Lions the Real McCoy' said the *Pretoria News*, whereas only three days earlier, after the narrowest of defeats by Northerns, we had been pussycats once more. South African confidence in the ability of their teams seemed like a rubber inflatable. Win, and it was all puffed up fit to bust, lose, and it deflated in seconds flat.

At the post-match press conference Geech and the Pink Salmon, both cock-a-hoop, broke their own rules and had a dig at the ref. 'We picked up the pace of the game very well in the second half, particularly as we got so few 50–50 decisions. If you defend well, isolate a player and turn him round you should get something for it. A number of times you could see the ball coming back on our side, yet they still got the put-in,' said Geech.

The Pink Salmon was even more pointed when he suggested, tongue-in-cheek, 'Personally, I'm thinking of citing the referee.'

A hard morning's training on Thursday – long and intense – before we departed for Durban and the last game in the 'Bermuda Triangle' against Natal did nothing to dampen the buzz from last night. No one was buzzing more than Bentos. He seemed to have been on a high ever since he had scored with his first touch against Border. Two more tries against Western Province had sent him into orbit, so who knew where he was heading after the effort against Gauteng.

Having spent seven years playing league, Bentos had never been on anything as big as a Lions tour. Consequently, as happens with really high-profile sports events, particularly if you're a bit of a character (and undoubtedly he is), everything to do with you – the way you play, eat, sleep and drink – gets enlarged through the eye of the media. You are seen and written about as never before. You are big – and if you are not used to it, you can get carried away with it. You can't help but be affected when you're the focus of that sort of attention, and Bentos was no different.

However, fair play to him, he did manage to keep his feet on the ground most of the time. In the changing rooms after the Gauteng game I congratulated him on a fantastic try but also reminded him of just how easy it was on a tour to go from a rooster one minute to a feather duster the next. After Western Province his next outing had been against Northerns, and he had a shocker. He was subbed not because he was exhausted but because he was playing that badly. He took it on the chin. But you can't keep a good man down. His next move was to tell the press conference that he had hung on to the ball because 'against Western Province, Jerry didn't pass to me, so I wasn't passing to him.'

Bentos did himself a lot more good than harm amongst the squad, and was at the heart of the social scene. However, as happens on tour, the wind-up merchants usually end up getting a bit of their own medicine. In Bentos's case it involved a letter to his wife that, allegedly, Tim Stimpson got hold of that contained the immortal line 'Luv, even I can't believe how bloody famous I am out here.' He was ripped into mercilessly. His first line of defence when I raised the issue was 'Now, would I say something like that, Jerry?' To which he got the reply 'Of course you would, Bentos, that's you all over.'

To make the transition to being one of the players of the tour from someone who before the tour was a controversial selection and something of an unknown quantity was quite an achievement. Bentos provided some special moments both on and off the field. He was good fun, and a good tourist.

Another player whose tour was made against Gauteng was Neil Back. Throughout the tour Backy was sensational, and, as I've said, his performance out wide against Mpumalanga had been one of the best by an openside I had ever seen. He doesn't get this freedom with Leicester because they don't play like the Lions. You don't see the best of Neil Back with them because their style doesn't bring his talent to the top. Nor do England play in a way that makes Neil Back look the world-class player that he is. But with the Lions, every time he played and the ball went wide, or anywhere for that matter, he was there. The bloke is the link – the missing link – for anyone who wants to play 15-man rugby. You can't play in that style without players like Backy. He was so good that size was a non-issue. I feel really pleased for him, because he answered his critics so completely that he earned the right to walk away from the tour smiling inwardly and outwardly. Nonetheless, I don't think it rewrites the past. He was left out by England because of the tighter game they wanted to play, which, given that objective at that time, was probably the right decision. As for the now, all I know is that whoever manages England is in a dream position with two opensides of the calibre of Backy and Richard Hill.

South Africa, meanwhile, had limbered up for the series against us by smashing Tonga 74–10 at Newlands on Tuesday night. It may have set a new Springbok record for a test win, but Carel du Plessis can't have learned a lot from the 12-try demolition. We certainly didn't. The mismatch was such that you couldn't help but feel for the Tongans, particularly as they appeared to have lost most of their impressive 1995 World Cup outfit to Aussie and New Zealand rugby. The match also left the South Africans with a few headaches. Du

Plessis's idea of keeping his squad out of the wars by withdrawing them from playing against the Lions for their provinces backfired when skipper Gary Teichmann, Small and Fritz van Heerden all picked up injuries.

Mind you, we didn't really need the game against Tonga to tell us about the Springboks because in Andy Keast we had an insider. A former full back, Keasty turned to coaching with Metropolitan Police and Harlequins after an injury-hit career finally ended in 1987. He had then gone to South Africa and earned his spurs as the Natal assistant director of coaching from 1994 to 1996, helping to master-mind their 1995 Currie Cup-winning campaign before returning to Harlequins.

His analysis of the Natal side meant that by the time Saturday arrived, the Lions knew more about Natal, who were the current Currie Cup holders, than they knew about themselves.

Seeing as I was surplus to requirements and Keasty also had a bit of time on his hands we had a few beers together on the Thursday evening, at TJ's, and Friday at Cottonfields, a little bistro just down the road from our hotel, the Beverly Hills, in the beach resort of Umhlanga.

Saturday, 14 June: British Isles v. Natal

Jayne phoned me at 7 a.m. She said not to worry, but she had just started having contractions. I phoned Fran and said that I wouldn't be making training that morning because my mind just wouldn't be on it. He agreed. In a sense it was quite good timing because I was a little bit hung over. I stayed in and waited for any more news from back home.

I then got ready to go to the game with the rest of the squad. We watched the first half from a hospitality box, but I then decided to go and join the boys on the bench so I could watch the game at pitch level.

Throughout the afternoon I was in constant touch with what was going on back at home by mobile phone. King's Park, Durban, to Bath in an instant. The wonders of modern technology. I got a blow by blow account of what was happening – that the midwife was coming to the house etc. – I spoke to my mum, I spoke to Jayne's mum. Initially I was phoning every half an hour and Jayne told me not to phone until 4 p.m., when the midwife was due. I phoned back and was told to try again at 5 p.m. I phoned and was told that Jayne was going into hospital and to phone back at 7 p.m. When I did, I was told that the birth was in progress and that everything was fine. Then, when I phoned back at 8 p.m. (7 p.m. UK time), the midwife told me that we had an 8lb 4oz baby daughter with lots of hair and in good nick and that Jayne, who had lost a bit of blood, was having a bath. An hour later I phoned Jayne, who was then back at home.

It was a strange feeling, although not as strange as it might have been to some, because I'd been through it before. I had been working in America when Holly, our second daughter, had been born.

I felt very happy and proud. It was a special moment. I was a Dad again. There's nothing more precious than a life, and seeing my first daughter, Imogen, being born is one of the most treasured moments in mine. Only a father who's watched his child being born knows what I mean.

However, I'm not one of those who gets all churned up about these things. Both Jayne and I knew that I was going to be away, and that was that. Of course I would have loved to have been there, but I've always been pretty down to earth. What's meant to be is meant to be, and it's a fact of life that I wasn't there when either Holly or Saskia, as we called our newest arrival, was born. I looked forward to holding Saskia in my arms, and knew that when I got back home it would be as if I had always been there.

While fatherhood had again been beckoning in my direction, the Lions, fittingly, had scored a mother and father of a victory over Natal. Unfortunately, it came at a price. Rob Howley, who had been a racing certainty to play scrum-half in the first test the following week, had to leave the pitch after having his shoulder dislocated in a tackle early in the match. It was the end of his tour.

Rob is such an honest player, such a dedicated trainer and such a talent that I really felt for him. Everybody in the squad respected him and he was just one week, one match away from fulfilling a dream. Most of his family were about to leave Wales to come out for the test. I was not surprised that there was a tear in his eye when we came to say our goodbyes.

However, although the British press were of the view that Rob's departure had dealt a real body blow to our chances in the test series, once again it did not mirror the feeling within the squad because Matt Dawson, who came on as a replacement at King's Park, had been playing out of his skin. He didn't let up against Natal.

Natal are called the Sharks. In this instance it was a case of the biter bit. They had no answer to anything we tried, whereas anything they tried we snuffed out to the extent that all they had on the scoreboard were four penalties from Gavin Lawless. In reply we scored three tries, through Gregor, Catty and Lol, and even though the last two came in the closing six minutes they were a fair reflection of our dominance.

There were a number of outstanding performances. Neil Jenkins took up where he left off against Gauteng to finish with a tally of 24 points with some near flawless goal-kicking, the scrum took their eight to the cleaners, and some of the tackling and carrying up of the ball was thunderous. On one occasion, Snake, raring to go after a combination of injury and ban, hurtled into the 20-stone Ollie Le

Roux and knocked him into the middle of next week. It put you in mind of what Asterix used to do to Roman legionaries. The back row of Lol, Richard Hill and Eric Miller gave Natal the hurry-up all afternoon, and Woody was everywhere – including putting in a clever chip-ahead which, when Woody was stiff-armed by Le Roux, Gregor pounced on to score. Later on Geech described his reaction to Woody's footballing skills as 'What the hell? – oh, well played!'

King's Park is a unique rugby venue, with a carnival atmosphere that puts the West car park at Twickenham in the shade. There are also some unique practices that I can't see being adopted by the RFU. One involved a group of models running on to the field in dressing-gowns and then slipping them off to reveal swimming costumes with initials that spelt the name of the sponsors, Canon, and the other was a remote-controlled motorized kicking tee transporter in the shape of a shark's fin which zipped on and off the field during play.

Before and after matches the stadium's surrounding acres of pitches are transformed into one massive open-air 'braii' (barbecue), and the Pink Salmon suggested that we go walkabout and savour the victory. The squad, all of whom had embraced each other after the final whistle, decided instead to head back to Umhlanga to hold a court session.

From there, Jase, Lol, Wiggy (Graham Rowntree) and myself went out to wet baby Saskia's head at Cottonfields.

We went secure in the knowledge that the Springboks, watching the game at their training camp in Cape Town, must have known in their hearts that the game the following week would be no cake-walk.

Chapter 9

CAPE CRUSADERS

Not playing leaves you in a bit of a limbo. Where you might get released from some of the pressures for a while, you take on the role of watching and waiting. It's an odd place to be because there's a whole host of emotions at play. You want everyone to do well, you want the side to do well and win, but you don't want to see your own chances going down the plughole. In a squad that isn't closely knit you could well become what Peter FitzSimons, the former Wallaby lock turned journalist, describes as 'A Deathrider', i.e. just waiting for one of your mates to bite the dust. However, I felt happy within myself, not because I knew I was in the test side – no one does for sure – but because I knew I couldn't do much more than I'd done. My only regret was not scoring against Gauteng, because that would almost certainly have signed and sealed it.

Although Geech had given me the nod the previous week, I still felt slightly uncomfortable. You can never be 100 per cent sure.

It had something to do with the 1989 Lions tour to Australia. Before the first test in Sydney, Roger Uttley had told me to go and get an early night, hinting that there would be good news. I did so only to get a call from Rog at 8 a.m. the following morning to apologize. He said that he should never have jumped the gun, and that I was on the bench. From that time on I have never taken any selection for real until I hear my name read out or see it on the teamsheet.

Another important difference between this and the other Lions tours I had been on was that by this stage everyone would have known pretty well what the test side was because the party would already have split into the Saturday side and the midweek team. This time there had been much more of a mix-and-match between midweek and Saturday sides, both of which had done well, and so there was a far greater degree of uncertainty.

The upshot was that the squad as a whole was buoyant, and had really knitted together in a common cause. It was a credit to the management that they had achieved one of their key objectives. The other was that we had emerged from the 'Bermuda Triangle' relatively unscathed.

Sunday was regeneration morning for the Saturday boys, but hard training for the rest of us at King's Park. Afterwards we headed for the airport for the flight to Cape Town. A long delay waiting for our

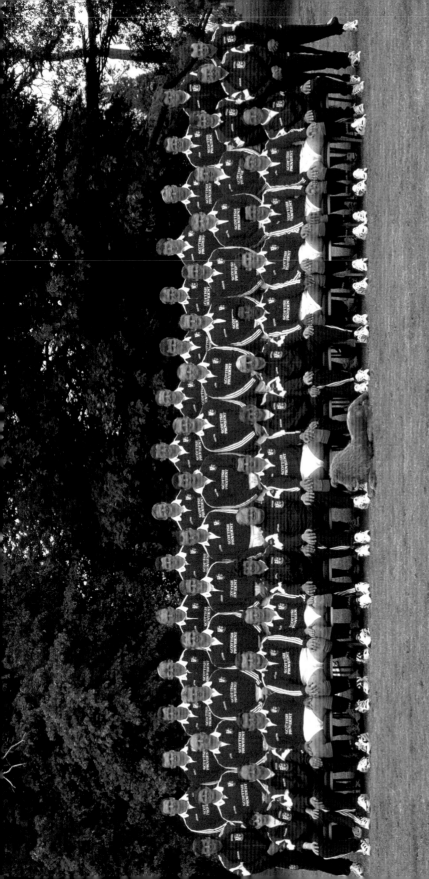

The British and Irish Lions. South Africa, 1997.

In full flight.

No way through this time.

adidas

SCOTTISH
ROVIDENT

Business as usual

The final whistle blows at the end of the second test in Durban.

Celebrating with Geech.

2 – 0. With Martin Johnson and Neil Jenkins, and the series won.

The battle lost, but the war won. The squad with the cup at the end of the third test. I missed out on these celebrations because of a broken arm during the match.

kit on arrival was followed by another bus breakdown – but when we got to our destination it was well worth it. Camps Bay is one of the most beautiful settings I've seen anywhere in the world and it plays host to one of my favourite restaurants, Blues. The food there is excellent, the atmosphere is totally relaxed and the view of the bay, with its golden beach and blue surf, is breathtaking. Besides my wife's cooking, Blues takes the biscuit. Out of this world.

After dinner the team to play the Emerging Springboks in Wellington was announced when we got back to the hotel in Newlands. Bentos was on the right wing. The look on his face said it all: 'Am I not in the test team, or what?'

However, Fran and Geech insisted to the players and the press that nothing should be read into the selection and that test places were still up for grabs. They were also insistent that the squad should concentrate only on the game in hand, and that those not playing at Wellington on Tuesday should help the guys in the team both on the training field and in the hotel. It was a good move because, by this stage, training and post-match analysis had been split according to the teams that had played in midweek and on Saturday. The next evening after every match the team that had played would go through the video assessment with Andy Keast, who had spent most of the night before making compilations of them in action, both in attack and defence.

The drums, meanwhile, have started to beat for the Boks in the local press – in a nutshell, they thought they were going to 'do' us up front. Apparently the Bok forwards are in a different league from the provincial combinations.

Tuesday, 17 June: British Isles v. Emerging Springboks

Bentos wouldn't lie down. He tried to gee up the side by saying that nothing was done and dusted with regards to test selection, but most of us knew that, whatever Fran and Geech had said in public, a large part of the test team had been pencilled in already. It would need something exceptional for someone to play themselves into con-tention.

Already rumours had started to circulate through the squad. It looked as if Jeremy Davidson, who had been selected over Simon Shaw for the Natal game but had then dropped out through injury, would spring a surprise, and that Tom Smith and Paul Wallace had stolen a march at prop.

There's always speculation – but no one bar those in on selection meetings ever knows. I caught a combi out to Wellington, which is in the Boland, a farming region about an hour's drive out of Cape Town. The place had the feel of a small agricultural town about it, and the stadium was pretty agricultural to boot. There was, however, a sizeable crowd and a lot of red-white-and-blue in evidence. The

Lions supporters had started to arrive in large numbers for the test series.

They gave the side plenty of support and couldn't have been disappointed when Jase led the side to a six-try victory, with Nick Beal claiming a hat-trick and Tim Stimpson hitting all six conversions. As had happened throughout the tour, the South Africans, a development side picked from outside the Springbok squad, were unable to live with the Lions when the ball was pushed wide and, again, crumbled in the last quarter.

That evening back at the Holiday Inn in Newlands a squad meeting was called where Fran told us that we would find out through an envelope under the door at 8 a.m. whether or not we had made the test side. Had a chat with the Doc in the lift afterwards about what the side might be – I told him that speculation was not my expert field! I had, however, been winding up Johno. I told him that I wasn't mucking about with all this envelope stuff, and that I would wait for the puff of white smoke to come out of the selectors' meeting and then give him a ring. I had no intention of doing so, but it was a way of blowing off steam. Kyran Bracken had just joined the Lions as a replacement for Rob Howley and had the pleasure of rooming with me.

In fact, the selection meeting didn't go on too long – one and a half to two hours. Johno mentioned later that it had not been a very pleasant experience. It can't be much fun having to tell blokes you've played with for much of the year with England and Leicester that they are surplus to requirements. It confirmed me in my belief that captaincy and me were never meant for each other.

D-Day. The white envelope arrived. I was in. I went down to breakfast and saw Shaggy Greenwood, whose greeting was 'Well done, you old sod.' Otherwise the dining-room was a bit eerie, too quiet. I could tell by looking at Bentos that he wasn't in. He had misery written all over his face. The whole atmosphere had me doubting whether I was in the side myself. The note had been so brief that I'd only glanced at it once before leaving the room – but I hadn't had the reassurance, the finality, of hearing my name read out in the traditional manner. I headed back up to the room and checked. I really was in. Hallelujah!

At 9 a.m. we all met in our groups from the Impact session in Weybridge with a view to letting those who were disappointed at the test selection have the opportunity to get it off their chests. My view was that it was unnecessary. No one had anything much to say, in fact we made a bit of a joke of it. I learned, however, that Bentos had aired his views a bit earlier.

One thing that had surprised me was that Bentos decided to carry a little camcorder around to do some filming for the 'fly-on-the-wall' documentary team that had access to us during the tour. Apparently that morning Bentos was up at 5 a.m. running a bath and preparing himself for the arrival of the envelope, filming himself along the way.

Then, when the envelope came under the door, there he was filming away saying, 'Now I'm opening the letter – Oh, bloody hell! I don't believe it!', and then going ballistic because he wasn't in the test side.

I don't know if it was an act or not, but because it was so alien to me I found it hard to take on board. I would never put myself in that sort of situation because it's not the sort of profile I want, or the perception I want other people to have of me. If that's Bentos, then fair enough. In some ways he and I were poles apart, but in others quite alike – for instance, like me he plays both the straight man and the funny man, and people can't always tell where we're coming from.

The white envelopes had ordained the following team: Neil Jenkins; Ieuan Evans, Scott Gibbs, Jerry Guscott, Alan Tait; Gregor Townsend, Matt Dawson; Tom Smith, Keith Wood, Paul Wallace, Martin Johnson (captain), Jeremy Davidson, Lawrence Dallaglio, Eric Miller, Richard Hill. Reserves: John Bentley, Austin Healey, Mike Catt, Barry Williams, Jason Leonard, Rob Wainwright.

The main talking points were the inclusion of the relatively light-weight Irish pairing of Paul Wallace and Jeremy Davidson in the pack over the heavyweight English duo of Jase and Simon Shaw, and the inclusion of Alan Tait, a centre, on the wing. The Newlands test would be the first time this team had played together on the tour.

At the press conference Fran and Geech stated that the test-selection process was the toughest they have ever been involved in because they could have made a case for selecting every player in the squad.

The team was not released until the following day. Next, we headed out to Stellenbosch, in the heart of the winelands 40 minutes outside Cape Town, for a murderous training outing. We had a full-on contact session – where we concentrated particularly on defending against the Springboks' short lineout – which lasted for two hours. Understandably some of those not selected for the test were carrying a lot of disappointment. Things were very physical. We went to the Château Libertas winery for lunch but, while the food was good, to me the whole object seemed to be defeated because we couldn't partake of what we could have drowned ourselves in. Wine. We then trudged back out, full of chicken pie, pudding and coffee, to do another set-piece and set-move session that nobody was up for. On the way back to Cape Town that evening the bus was the quietest it had been all tour. We were out on our feet. It had been a hell of a day.

Got back to learn that Eric Miller, who was selected as the test no. 8, had been ruled out by flu and replaced by Tim Rodber. The Doc warned us against taking flu medicine that might contain banned substances because Eric's father had given him some non-prescription stuff which, had he been drug-tested, would have seen him banned for a year.

The South African propaganda machine was working overtime. Johan Roux, the Gauteng and former Springbok scrum-half, had weighed in with: 'The Springboks will be another level up, a level I don't believe the Lions will cope with. After Saturday they will know what southern-hemisphere rugby is about.' Mark Andrews, who was due to front up to Martin Johnson, warned: 'I have heard a lot about Johnson. I just hope he can live up to what is written about him. He could get very demoralized if it doesn't work out.' All we heard was that they were going to be bigger, faster and stronger and play at a tempo we couldn't match.

Mind you, if they had seen the way we trained on the Thursday, they would probably have been even more bullish. I was frustrated with Gregor. I felt he had every right to be a free spirit, but not at the expense of the rest of the backline. There was a collective responsibility that he did not seem able to subscribe to – he seemed to have too many things on his mind. The fact that we were knackered from the Wednesday session didn't help, and though we improved gradually – the encouragement from the midweek backline proved to be crucial – we did not reach the standards that we set for ourselves.

Having paid a visit in the afternoon to Diamond World, where I bought gifts for Jayne and the kids, including a bracelet charm for little Saskia, I shook off the blues by going to Blues in the evening with Lol, Jase, Snake and Bentos. We decided to call it a day after three bottles of wine because it was starting to taste too good. The last thing any of us needed was a big night.

Friday was quiet, the weight of expectation was all around. The first test was the following day and this just hung over everyone.

There was no training, so I got up late, had a light lunch and then went for a tea excursion to the Botanical Gardens with the rest of the test team. Very British, I thought. At 6.30 p.m. the test squad met, split into units – the front five, the back row and half-backs, the midfield (Snake and me), and the back three – and talked calmly through our aims. There was now no more we could do before preparation became reality. Dinner wasn't up to much, so we adjourned to the team room to play snooker and watch *Blackadder* videos.

FIRST TEST (NEWLANDS, CAPE TOWN)

Saturday, 21 June: South Africa 16 British Isles 25

'Do or Die at Newlands' was how it was billed on the front page of the local rag that morning – and there was no doubt who the locals thought were going to be dead and buried at the end of it. In my heart of hearts I knew they were wrong: in terms of the quality of the players and the quality of the preparation the Lions were at least the Springboks' equal.

We had been reminded of that forcefully the previous evening. Geech had arranged for a video to be compiled in the UK putting together some of the highlights of the tour to date, with music, the theme being 'How the Lions are Seen Back Home'. It had been flown out especially. It was uplifting to see yourselves scoring tries, making and breaking tackles, making breaks. There was a little cameo on everyone in the squad – all 35, not just the team. The 'Feelgood Factor' at work. It was a clever move.

I'm not a big routine man when it comes to build-ups, in the sense that I don't have too many habits that I stick to religiously. But on reflection there are a few more than I thought.

Generally I'll have a late light breakfast – cornflakes, toast and honey, coffee. Then we'd have a light team run-out, in tracksuits and trainers, where the backs will walk through their moves, and the forwards go through their lineout drills. I'll then go back to my room, pack my kit, and have a shave – mainly because I can't be bothered to after the match – and a shower, get changed into blazer etc., and listen to some music. About 15 minutes before the squad meeting I'd get down to the team room and play a bit of pool.

On the bus I always like to sit on the right-hand side, I don't know why. I also like to have a chat, which I find relaxing, and maybe a bit of a laugh, unlike some of the guys who just stick the head-phones on and cut themselves off. My only other quirk, apart from the bus, is that I have a pair of 'lucky' swimming trunks that I've worn for games for the past five or six years – but I'm not super-stitious enough to go the whole hog try to keep the same shirt, shorts and socks like some of the boys.

That routine was pretty much the one I followed before the first test. Then Fran addressed the full squad of 35. He stressed the importance of winning the first test in any series, how it gave you the essential psychological edge, and then read out messages of support from home and a few inspirational words from Shakespeare. The messages from home do tend to concentrate the mind on the fact that there are people out there four-square behind you. In this instance, there was a message from the former Great Britain and Wigan full back, Joe Lydon, proving that support for the Lions transcended the great divide between league and union. The Shakespeare went over my head. Fran, as is his way, tended to finish much of what he had to say with the stock phrase 'Simple as that'. He added, 'All the best,' and walked out with the remainder of the squad.

Then Geech took the floor. His message was that we should go out and be prepared to stretch the bounds. Throughout the tour he had encouraged us to try things, to play a 15-man game, and, he said, there was no better arena to do it in than Newlands. He added that the South Africans still had no respect for us, and produced a cardboard newspaper flyer with the words: 'Lions in town – the "Pansies" have arrived.'

However, in my experience it's the individual himself who provides most of the motivation, not outside forces. My method is to convince myself that I have to play well. I don't take a lot of convincing.

I tell myself you have to enjoy yourself and the only way you're going to do that is if you're relaxed and go where instinct takes you.

Like the advertising slogan says, 'Just do it!' I'm not into visualizing techniques (i.e. imagining yourself doing well) like some of the lads, but I always take 20 seconds just to sit down and shut everything out and then I repeat my 'relax, enjoy' mantra.

I don't think I'm the most nervous of players, but sometimes I get this horrible, empty feeling in the pit of my stomach which tells me it's high time to get out there. Some of the boys get so wound up they start retching, and there's a lot of twitching goes on as we go through our various routines for handling the nerves. But overriding all that for me is a sense of excitement.

Newlands was one of the other things I liked about Cape Town. Unlike some of the concrete monsters built in Britain it actually looks good. Because it's not that huge – there was a full house of 51,000 for the match – and there are so many corporate hospitality boxes, it hasn't got the most intimidating of atmospheres. You didn't get the feeling of outright hostility that I've experienced at Murrayfield, where you just sense that the whole of Scotland is against you, and at Cardiff Arms Park where the crowd almost overhangs the pitch. Even the staff in the Newlands Holiday Inn were wishing us well, and there was no doubt in my mind that many of them were sincere.

It was only a five-minute bus ride from the hotel to the stadium but along the way we soaked up some of the atmosphere as we passed the supporters. It was amazing just how many Lions fans had made the journey from Britain and Ireland to support us. Inevitably, they were significantly outnumbered – but never came close to being outsung – by the Springbok supporters. The thumbs down signs from the locals – and various others of a less savoury nature – and their nursery-rhyme T-shirts with the words 'Fee-Fi-Foh-Fum, I smell the blood of an Englishman' left us in no doubt what they were hoping for, but, instead of adopting the ramrod back and stony-eyed stare of some of the boys, I looked at them and laughed. It was good to feed off their hostility.

As soon as we got to the ground I changed and went on to the pitch to savour the atmosphere in the stadium. Then, as always, I warmed up thoroughly for about 35 minutes, stretching, running and kicking the ball before returning to the changing room for the final build-up.

The forwards and backs split with Johno and Woody taking the forwards into the shower area for a four-letter word psyching-up seminar – the fly-on-the-wall documentary crew must have thought all their birthdays had come at once. The backs, who were within earshot of the expletives, had some difficulty keeping straight faces. But the tension was such that it didn't last any longer than the forming of the team huddle before we took the pitch.

Then came the feeling. It had struck before during the tour, but there was a sense above all others as we bonded into a huddle before running out to the Newlands roar. As I looked around the other faces I felt a deep confidence in them – there was no one who made me think 'He's not up to it.' It's a sense deep inside that you know you can win. It's a feeling I had not experienced since Bath's heyday. There was that much belief.

A bit of shouting in the tunnel, my routine jog into the opposition half and rubbing of dirt on my hands, another huddle, the new South African anthem, and it was on.

There's no doubt in my mind that despite the drama of the last seven minutes when we scored tries through Matt Dawson and Alan Tait to clinch the game, it wasn't a great spectacle to watch. Nor was it one of the great games to play in. But it was a great occasion, and a great result. In addition, the try by Daws was a peach. To beat Ruben Kruger for pace off the back of an attacking Lions scrum and then sucker Gary Teichmann, André Venter and Joost van der Westhuizen with a superb dummy is no mean feat. Most of my appreciation of it is based on seeing the video afterwards because at the time, at ground level, it was hard to figure out exactly what had happened. All I can remember is that he went and then he darted through this forest of bodies, scored and then disappeared. I wondered where the hell he was. Then I caught a glimpse of him over in the corner doing a little football-style celebration.

I was soon aware that it was not going to be the sort of game where I was going to see much of the ball. In fact, I didn't get my first touch until the test was 30 minutes old, and in all touched the ball three or four times in the whole game. If we are brutally honest about the game we did not play good attacking rugby for much of it – and a big part of the problem was that Ieuan Evans, Alan Tait, Neil Jenkins and myself all saw so little of the ball. We were frustrated on two counts: first, the Springboks got away with killing a fair amount of our ball, and second, we were passing it one less time than we should have done with too many 'macho' runs being made. We got suckered into the 'In, Smash' game too much – which is meat and drink to the South Africans – rather than moving the ball into space.

Until Daws's try, which gave us a 20–16 lead, we had been kept in the game by a combination of excellent goal-kicking by Jenks, who finished with five penalty successes from six attempts, and tremendous defence. Although the South Africans scored tries through Os du Randt and new full back Russell Bennett, the big hits coming from the likes of Scott Gibbs, Tim Rodber and Lawrence Dallaglio were shaking them up despite their bulk. In fact, the defence was so punishing I was left wondering how some of them got back up. In the case of Japie Mulder, their powerful centre, an attempt to turn the tables with a thunderous tackle on Lol Dallaglio backfired when, although Lol was winded, Mulder damaged his shoulder. He played no further part in the series.

In many ways the first test was a mirror image of the lessons we had learned up to that point, in particular that South African sides were vulnerable in the final quarter. Our last try came courtesy of a burst up the side of a scrum by Daws and Tim Rodber. It was followed by a ruck and a blasting run by Gibbsy, and was rounded off by a passing movement featuring Rodders and Jenko before 'Pidge' Tait touched down. I can still see 'Pidge' celebrating in front of the crowd, using his hands as if they were six-shooters, and then coming back and high-fiving the rest of us.

It felt good to have lowered the colours of so many of the media cynics, both South African and British, and to have earned the respect of the Springboks. They should never have been gullible enough to believe their own press. As Pidge said after the game, 'The main thing that came out of this was respect. We earned it.'

No one had earned it more than the two lightweight props, Tom Smith (16st 7lb) and Richard Wallace (17st 7lb), who had been widely tipped to be pulverized by their massive Bok counterparts, the 20-stone du Randt and the 18-stone Adrian Garvey. After creaking at the first couple of scrums, they settled impressively and in the last 15 minutes had the Boks backpedalling. Brilliant. It had been a huge physical effort all round, but theirs reaped the greatest reward that day because one of the biggest psychological weapons in the South African armoury had been disarmed.

However, although the crucial first test was ours – traditionally the side who won it took the series – there was no riotous celebration, no champagne, no nothing apart from slaps on the back for Daws and Pidge. Even then some of the steam was drawn because they had been nabbed by TV as soon as they came off the pitch. The changing room was far from the noisiest I've known. There was still the sense of a job half done.

Back at the hotel the Lions phoned home. The word across the airwaves was one of congratulations and a great deal of excitement. That night we had dinner and a few beers in the Cantina Tequila, but the mood in the squad was one of unfinished business. If it had been a two-test series we would at least have known we couldn't lose. But it wasn't, and King's Park, Durban, was only a week away. However, I needed to unwind and I organized a combi to take myself, Jase and Lol to a bistro called the Café Verdi. From there we went and drank a few Jack Daniel's and coke in a nightclub called Sirens before heading back late.

Chapter 10

A DROP FOR THE DEAD DONKEYS

The South African reaction to losing the first test was hysterical in all senses of the word. 'Hold the front page!' seemed to have been the cry after the defeat of the beloved Boks. The South African *Sunday Times* carried a massive block headline of earth-shattering proportions – 'Boks: What Went Wrong' – and then a six-point plan for putting things right.

I was sure there would be more to come. But the one thing this knee-jerk press reaction overlooked was the depth of our determination and the level of our preparation. They found it hard to accept that we had soaked up everything they could throw at us through good defence and then counter-punched to score two good tries. The truth was that we knew their game inside out. Geech and Keasty had pressed exactly the right buttons. However, the Lions got the impression from reading the South African press that the Springbok problems were all self-inflicted, they were still the better side, and that somehow we were divorced from the process. They couldn't have been more wrong.

There were three glaring examples. First, and most obvious, was the way they assumed that the scrummage would be our Achilles heel despite the fact that we were a touring side with time to remedy any ills. The Boston Strangler and Wally had answered Jim Telfer's call to 'Hold the world!' Second, our defence was outstanding. Instances like one Rodders tackle which almost cut Henry Honiball – who they call 'The Blade' – in half, and another where Gibbsy dumped Bennett, help to lift your own side and sink the opposition.

Third, they were as predictable and naive a side as you get at international level in the sense that they felt they would always be able to smash a way through. Their only problem was, when that didn't work, nothing changed. The irony was that, when they did move the ball wide, they were dangerous. South Africa expect to bust up, halt and roll over the opposition. If they expect teams to fold and crumble these days, they've got another think coming. They are what they are – simple. They play simple rugby. Nor was their defence as strong as we anticipated, because they were not as fit as we had expected them to be.

They were also very much a side based on individuals. For example, while Joost van der Westhuizen is a very good player, he has a few flaws, one of which is that he always looks for himself first. Honiball is similar, and they based a lot of their game on him getting past the gain-line and unloading to the back row or Japie Mulder. If Honiball wasn't functioning and Mulder was out – as he was after his collision with Lol – two main components of their team were missing. I thought Honiball probably had a lot more to offer, but the only variations in his game seemed to be pass to Mulder or try to crash through himself. Weird considering that they were not a team that lacked backline talent.

Despite the shell-shocked South African reaction to defeat, we had no doubts about either our own qualities or that we deserved to win because of them. In a sense we had done to them what they did to the All Blacks in winning the 1995 World Cup final. We had nullified their strengths and then put ourselves in a position to win. The Lions squad had adopted 'Wonderwall' by Oasis as their tour song. Now the Springboks and their supporters knew why.

On the Sunday we had a hard training session at Villagers in the morning, packed and left for Durban. This time our destination was one of the big, spacious, beachfront Holiday Inns rather than Umhlanga, although we did head that way later that evening for dinner in Langoustines. No prizes for guessing that it is a fish restaurant.

Come Monday morning the gunbarrels of the South African rugby press had been pointed at Carel du Plessis. All I can say is our Five Nations coaches don't know how lucky they are. Some of the stuff was savage.

The outrage at the 25–16 defeat was such that du Plessis's two immediate predecessors as Springbok coach weighed into him no holds barred. André Markgraaff, sacked for making racist remarks only a few months before, used his syndicated newspaper column to lash his successor. 'Complacency, overconfidence and a non-existent game plan all contributed,' huffed Markgraaff. Not to be outdone, Kitch Christie, the 1995 World Cup-winning coach, slammed the Springboks for being unfit, patternless and leaderless: 'We seem to have gone back to the late 1980s where the fly-half couldn't link properly with his loose forwards,' said Christie.

However, neither of them could match the stuff aimed at du Plessis by sections of the South African rugby media. Mark Keohane, writing in the *Cape Times*, was a real poison-pen merchant. 'The most positive aspect of Saturday's result was that the powers that be now know that their decision to appoint du Plessis was not a moment of inspiration, but one of madness,' said Keohane. 'Du Plessis has been shown up for bringing a kindergarten mentality into the battle-hardened playground of test rugby . . . he has taught them nothing more than rugby's equivalent of suicide,' he added.

All this for a side that matched the Lions two tries to two and was leading until the last seven minutes. It left you wondering where these guys would go, should South Africa lose again in Durban. To hire an AK47?

The side to go on the day trip the next day to Bloemfontein to play Free State, the last of the Super 12 provinces, was announced with Ollie Redman named as captain. He looked like the cat that had got the cream – if that doesn't sound too far-fetched for a 6ft 4in slaphead with surgical scars from head to toe.

Tuesday, 24 June: British Isles v. Free State

For the first time on tour the party split up. It had been decided early in the tour that the team that played Free State would not be accompanied by the rest of the squad preparing for the second test. However, the Pink Salmon and Geech insisted that there were still opportunities to make the test side.

The 'shadow' test squad was up early for a two-hour training session after which we went and saw the midweek team off as they headed for Bloemfontein. I was delighted not to be traipsing all the way up there, much as I wanted to see Ollie and the team do well. It was a good call by the management.

The boys didn't seem to miss us too badly. In fact, it was one of the finest performances of the tour, and as a total team performance it was the best. That evening we watched the game live on TV and the first thing that struck me was that it was played at such terrific pace it seemed as if someone had pressed the fast-forward button. The Lions played a complete 15-man game, total rugby, and mastered the art that Geech had been trying to instil in us of releasing the ball just before contact – and, if it was taken in at all, it came back very quickly. They did it so well that they ran in seven tries – three of them from Bentos – and Catty could play it as he wanted to. I almost yearned to be in Bloem. It was the sort of game I would have loved to have played in.

As for Bentos, it seemed to me that he was out to prove a point. Most of us realized by this time that, if Bentos got anything like a sniff of the line, there was no way anybody was going to get a pass. He got wrapped up once with two men outside him and for his second try used Batman, who was better placed to score, as a decoy. Bentos was desperate to get into the test side.

Then there was Ollie. I was so pleased for him. For a man who had been discarded by England so many times and told he was too small to play lock at that level it must have been a dream come true to captain the Lions to a record win over such powerful opposition. He told me afterwards he was just so relieved that it had turned out all right on the night.

It was just the fillip the test squad needed in the build-up to the big one at King's Park.

The guys got back from Bloem late so training on Wednesday didn't start until 1 p.m. The bad news was that Shaggy Greenwood's tour was over after he sustained both concussion and shoulder damage in a tackle towards the end of a game in which, with his straight lines of running, he had played a blinder. It was a great pity, but I have no doubt at all that England and the Lions have not heard the last of him.

More bad news followed during training, when Ieuan Evans pulled a groin muscle which the Doc immediately assessed as needing a six-week lay-off. Like they say, one man's ceiling is another man's floor – and it looked like Bentos was about to be on top.

A conversation with Geech before Ieuan was actually injured, where he asked me how I felt both Ieuan and Bentos were playing, indicated to me that the selectors were considering Bentos's claims in any case. My own view is that they would probably not have changed a winning side, because we had seen very little attacking ball out wide and had held up well in defence.

We trained pretty well all afternoon. At one stage Pidge Tait suggested that we use the rugby-league practice of calling out the names of the opposition to help our own communications when we're defending. The rest of us had a bit of a laugh about it – 'Joubert!', 'Honiball!', 'Van der West . . . Oh, dear, his name's so long he's just scored.' In the end we didn't take Pidge's advice and the defensive calls were, as ever, the tried and trusted 'Yours!' or 'Mine!'

There's no doubt that there were things we were able to learn from the rugby-league boys in the squad, but ultimately when it came to playing rugby union at this level there was more that they needed to learn from us than vice versa.

*

Thursday morning began with the white envelope under the door. There were no surprises, the only change from the first test being Bentos for Ieuan. It was followed by a two-hour training session – our last before the test – and in the afternoon, after the team press interviews, I played golf with Jase, Austin Healey and Nick Beal before a team dinner at Langoustines. Friday was a day off. The Lions supporters were camped in the hotel in large numbers, but for the most part they were not too demanding – the only time they can be a pain in the backside is occasionally when they get too drunk to accept that they're drunk.

Surprise, surprise, the South African papers were predicting a Springbok backlash but our confidence was sky-high. The win on Saturday had strengthened the Lions' self-belief massively. My mum, Susan, arrived in Durban in time for one of the biggest days of my rugby life. It was great to see her there.

SECOND TEST (KING'S PARK, DURBAN)

Saturday, 28 June: South Africa 15 British Isles 18

If anyone was nervous, no one was showing it. The whole feel around the squad was one of relaxed confidence. I had a very enjoyable breakfast with mum and saw my first photos of Saskia.

An adorable, wrinkled little prune. Then it was down to business.

The atmosphere in the team room that morning was something else. There was music pumping out of a juke-box so loud that by the time you'd put your bag down the beat had overwhelmed you. People were singing along, even doing a bit of dancing – and all there was to drink was water. In all my international experience I'd never known anything like it. If Jack Rowell had heard something like that before an England match he'd have thought we were all off our heads.

I'd been sharing a room with Neil Jenkins, which was useful because, like me, he's a bit of a chocaholic. Like all goal-kickers he had a lot of pressure to deal with, but you wouldn't believe it to look at him. He loves a drink and he and Carcass (Mark Davies, the physio) were for ever betting that one could drink the other under the table. I used to rib him a bit because he talks to himself in such a broad Welsh accent that it's hard to work out what he's on about. He's a tidy bloke and meticulous, like his kicking. He did additional kicking training for about an hour a day throughout and, given the measure of his contribution to the tour, is about as unassuming as they come. When it was all over we were quite chuffed that our room had supplied all the points – and, believe me, they weren't easy to come by. Jim Telfer had predicted that the Springboks would throw everything at us, including the kitchen sink, and he was right.

Perhaps they had been inspired by these words from Obed Mlaba, the mayor of Durban, on the morning of the match: 'The Amabokoboko will win because they learned their lesson in Cape Town. They've come to the champion rugby city and there's no way they can lose because we don't want the city's name to be tarnished.'

Fran Cotton was not about to be outdone by the mayor. When Fran addressed us at the squad meeting after our run-out and stretch on the beach front, he had obviously given his speech plenty of thought. After exhorting us not to let the chance of rugby immortality slip through our fingers, there was a dramatic pause as he let it sink in. He then referred us to those famous words of Napoleon that 'we all' knew. There was a further dramatic pause, but this time an unscheduled one, as Fran was forced to remind himself of those words by looking down at the piece of paper he had written them on. I can't even remember now what they were because at the time I was desperately choking back the disgraceful guffaw which, had it broken through, would have completely detonated the air of solemn determination in that room. It wasn't disrespect, it was simply funny – and there's nothing like knowing you can't laugh to make you want to laugh.

The atmosphere at King's Park was electric, a cross between a carnival and an away Five Nations match because there were so many supporters in red-white-and-blue chanting, 'Lions! Lions!' – as many as 8000 – among the massed ranks of Bok supporters in their green and gold.

Before the match Gibbsy was like a man in unshakeable pursuit of a mission. On the eve of the test he had given a TV interview in which he said, 'The whole of the British Isles and Europe is behind us – all 21 of us will give it our all as if it was World War Three.'

'I'm sure that if we have to defend for two-thirds of the game to win it, we'll relish it,' he added. The words were prophetic. As the deafening wall of sound hit us when we ran on to the pitch and we went into the huddle before the Boks ran out, Gibbsy was in the middle jabbing his finger. 'No step backwards! We're not walking off this pitch having lost. This is ours!' There are some players who, when they say something, you know that it is meant. There is a time when something is in your heart which communicates itself to others. They know it is sincere because they share it, and then you get the collective will that says, 'We've got to make it happen.'

Now was the hour, and Gibbsy was a catalyst in one of the greatest defensive performances in the history not only of the Lions, but of international rugby. The Springboks came at us like men possessed, but we just kept knocking them down, getting up and making another tackle and another. It was unbelievable, with Gibbsy, Tim Rodber and Lol Dallaglio all making huge hit after huge hit. The Springboks won 70 per cent of all the possession in the first hour and, although Jenko kept us in the game with his immaculate goal-kicking, van der Westhuizen's close-range try and then Montgomery's just after half-time after Pidge's wayward pass had us under the cosh. Pidge wasn't alone in making a mistake. Bentos went high on Joubert and his expert hand-off let them in for a third. However, if I hadn't coughed up the ball in the tackle just prior to that – I simply got my body in an awkward position and then made the mistake of trying to move it rather than hold on to it – Joubert wouldn't have got his chance.

At half-time when, against the run of play, we led 6–5, Jim Telfer had exhorted us, in his own unique way, to 'Kill them. Kill them till they're dead!' Given the two tries that they scored after the break, in most instances it would have been us that were dead. However, the will of the side was unbreakable. Gibbsy proved as much when, in a rare break-out, he steamed through the tackle of Os du Randt, knocking him into the middle of next week. On his way back I heard him say to du Randt, 'Get up, you fat ox.' We knew that we could take them if we lifted the siege and, gradually as the game approached our favourite quarter after the hour, our refusal to submit paid off as we came off the ropes to win the day.

We were fortunate when the ice-cool Jenko got the chance to level the scores with his fifth penalty from five attempts after Woody had appeared to knock on immediately before Teichmann was penalized for handling in a ruck. But a good side makes its own luck. It stayed with us when Daws fed me that fateful ball to strike the drop-goal cleanly between the posts with six minutes remaining.

When I scored the try in the second test against Australia in 1989 I had an extraordinary sensation of a flashback in which the whole of my rugby life was rerun in three seconds. This time there was no rerun. It was replaced by a sense of disbelief. I couldn't believe it had fallen to me to do it – and that I'd actually managed to. I don't mind if it's talked about for a while and earns me a few free dinners, but please ask me to put a sock in it if I ever start attributing it to the cool, calculating edge bestowed on me by experience.

We held on, and gave them nothing until the final whistle trilled. Then there was mayhem. Everyone was hugging everyone else. Bentos came over, Gibbsy was there, we were all yelling, 'Yes! Yes! Yes!' We went and saluted the Lions supporters, who were raising the roof.

There are very few moments in my life when I've been happier than I was in that press conference at King's Park. Now I knew I could face the judges of rugby careers and know that they could never touch me.

Chapter 11

A BRIDGE TOO FAR

The party went on until dawn. It started back at the hotel with the ceremonial shaving of Geech's head by Woody. Geech had made the rash promise somewhere along the line that, if we won the series, he would sit in the barber's chair and submit to the crew-cut favoured by some of the boys. Afterwards he became known as 'Roland Rat'.

There was a three-word entry in my diary for Sunday, 29 June: 'Just a blur.' But I know that throughout the blur there was a fixed smile on my face which said that life couldn't get much better.

But life often seems to have a way of balancing things out and by that evening we had found our way back up to the industrial area around Jo'burg known as the Vaal Triangle. Specifically, a place called Vanderbijlpark and a hotel called the Riverside on the Vaal river.

Once again, I thought we had taken a wrong turn off the planet. We were out in the middle of nowhere with nothing to do. If it had been 1 – 1 we could have been driven to despair, because all we could have done was mull over what had happened. It would have torn me to bits. We had just achieved something historic and I was surprised that there was no contingency plan in place to put us in one of the top Jo'burg hotels like the Sandton Sun, or even get us to a game park for 36 hours. It would not have deflected us one bit from our bid to inflict the first-ever home series whitewash on South Africa.

Because of the boredom factor there was always a slightly eerie feeling about what was called 'Whitewash Week'. However, we were professional to the end. The only problem is that it doesn't matter how professional you are if you know that the job has already been done. Just as the New Zealanders had found the year before, it was hard to raise the same motivation. The only way you could do it is to block out that you had won – and that is impossible.

Tony Stanger, who was touring South Africa with Scotland, was brought into the squad to replace Ieuan Evans and was awarded the famous red shirt with the crest of the four Home Unions. At the beginning of every tour over the course of the first two games every new Lion is called out, one by one in front of the rest of the squad, to receive his jersey. It is a unique tradition and the ceremony is repeated when a replacement joins the squad. Tony was the last of the replacements on the '97 tour but I'm sure that, like me, it is a moment he will never forget.

Tuesday, 1 July: British Isles v. Northern Free State

On Tuesday, most of us travelled two hours by coach to Welkom to see the midweek side, which, given the number of injuries, featured a handful of third test candidates. They emerged comfortable winners over a side nicknamed the Purple People Eaters. The only thing the Purples ate is dust as Tony Underwood ran in a hat-trick in the first quarter, although the Lions did allow them a late rally. Despite a good result, and the continued commitment of the squad, it was difficult to shake the feeling that the war was won.

The England contingent of the party was due to head for Australia immediately after the tour for a one-off test. I decided that, despite the invitation to join them, I would be heading home to see my family and phoned to tell Jack Rowell that was the case. Normally this would have been a hard decision, despite the fatigue everyone on the Lions tour felt, but Saskia's birth made my mind up.

I never thought I'd hear myself say, 'Jo'burg, at last,' but I said it as we landed in the Sandton Crowne Plaza in preparation for our final visit to Ellis Park and the heart of Afrikanerdom. We prepared well for the third test over the next couple of days, but there was a degree of disruption because we were unsure who was or wasn't fit. In the end Alan Tait, Gregor Townsend, Tim Rodber (who was laid low with gastric flu on the eve of the test) and Keith Wood were declared unfit and replaced by Tony Underwood, Mike Catt, Rob Wainwright (at no. 6 and Lol at no. 8) and Mark Regan, while Neil Back was preferred to Richard Hill at openside.

THIRD TEST (ELLIS PARK, JOHANNESBURG)

Saturday, 5 July: South Africa 35 British Isles 16

Come the day, the Lions were more than up for this one – being in the heartland made sure of that – and we wanted to win in style. We felt that in the test series we had only shown glimpses of the running game we had unleashed against provincial opposition.

Unfortunately it didn't happen for us, but it was a much closer game than the score indicated and one in which we gave as good as we got, particularly up front. However, this time South Africa had selected a goal-kicker at fly-half in Jannie de Beer and he proceeded to show them what they had missed out on in the first two tests.

I made a break in the first half where, with Neil Back inside me, I threw a speculative pass the other way and put us in trouble. I should have done the easy thing because Backy, as I've said elsewhere, was a revelation. He thoroughly deserved his cap because his work rate was simply phenomenal. My inability to find him was typical of how difficult it is for a side that hasn't played together before to marry things up.

The other break that occurred was to my left arm just above the wrist. It happened 30 seconds before half-time, with the Lions trailing 13−9. I was trying to get up in support of the ball when my opposite number, Danie van Schalkwyk, pulled me back by the shirt. I clipped him with my arm and soon afterwards lost the grip in my hand. I watched the rest of the game in hospital, where I had to go for X-rays.

With Jenko kicking his goals and Matt Dawson scoring his second try of the series in response to tries by Montgomery and van der Westhuizen the Lions were within reach of the Boks at 23−16 with 13 minutes remaining. You had the sense that the South Africans might just crumble again but, fair play to them, they came back well to score two more tries through Snyman and Rossouw and earned our respect by having hearts big enough to do so.

We had no complaints. As far as the Lions were concerned it works like this: if you should have won, you would have won.

It was sad to miss the team receiving the series trophy and parading it around the pitch, although it must have been a slightly odd feeling for Johno and the boys doing so after we had just been beaten. When I looked at Johno after the game, his face looked as if it had been through a blender, given all the cuts and bruises.

Martin Johnson was my sort of captain. He was a good communicator within the squad and, although he didn't talk all the time, what he said made sense. I'm one of those people who is inspired more by deeds than by words, and Johno is one of those types who, if he said follow me, you would. He went through so much pain it is untrue. He didn't play for the first couple of weeks because of a dicky shoulder and he had a long-standing groin injury throughout the tour.

Johnson is as tough as teak, a superb forward. He may even have surprised himself with some short, sweet, eloquent after-match speeches. He did well with the press but would not be too diplomatic if he felt we were being put upon. If he was named as the next England captain it would come as no surprise. He did nothing wrong, everything right.

He'd led a fiercely committed Lions squad with a self-belief that we all shared. In the end, the whitewash proved out of reach, but we'd won the series. We'd achieved what we set out to do and proved the doubters wrong.

Training took on a new meaning on the Sunday after the third test as we adjourned to a bar in Sandton called the Bushranger for an all-day drinking session. On the Monday the England lads headed for Oz and we were winging our way back home in Virgin upper class. Broken arm or not, home was where I wanted to be. No one wants to lose a cap but rugby doesn't always come first, and I had a baby daughter I wanted to see.

In fact it was my 32nd birthday, Jenko's was the next day and my mum was on the same flight. The party wasn't over. The next thing we knew the air stewardesses brought out a cake for me and Jenko. There was also a marker pen flying about the cabin and Woody, asleep, ended up getting a road map drawn on his face. When he woke up he chatted to the rest of us normally enough until he caught sight of himself in the toilet mirror.

Although at that very moment Woody might not have agreed, Lions tours are about bonding together. As a touring side you are always up against it. Success depends on whether you come together or you split into factions. The 1997 Lions came together very strongly. Playing with that squad I knew we were going to win games in the way that I used to at Bath. There were times with this Lions squad when we felt invincible – that we could take on the whole world and beat them.

When we landed at Heathrow the press were there in force and one of the things they were after was a photo of Saskia and me. As soon as the automatic doors opened Holly and Imogen ran out to greet me and I went over to Jayne and Saskia, who was asleep. Then, once the photocalls and press conference were over, and after the farewells to my team-mates – mostly 'see you', because we know we will – we got to the car park.

No sooner had I closed the car door than Saskia was crying, and Imogen and Holly both hollering at me at the same time. I said to Jayne, 'I've been away eight weeks, but it seems like eight hours.' There's nothing like a family to keep your feet on the ground.

EPILOGUE

The 1997 tour to South Africa reflected the start of a new era. It was the first professional tour by a British Isles side and the media attention was bigger than ever before. It was also, crucially, more professional in terms of the fact that this was the fittest, best-prepared Lions squad there has ever been. It had to be, otherwise we would not have survived.

By comparison with the rugby the 1997 Lions played, the stuff we produced in Australia in 1989 was appalling. The 1989 approach was pragmatic – a means to an end based on the fact that we had the stronger pack. On this tour things were far more proactive because the players had a far bigger input than on other Lions tours. We went on to the field playing the game we were comfortable with, and if the coaches asked us to do something we were not comfortable with, there were characters who told them. Back in 1989, if I had piped up as a 23-year-old and said, 'Lads, we're playing the game wrong,' with blokes like Ackford, Moore and Richards around, then I wouldn't have been flavour of the month.

In 1989 and in New Zealand in 1993 Geech acknowledged that our strength was with our forward domination. But I know now that, if he could have brought on the backs more, he would have, particularly in 1993. His problem was that there were too many big characters among the forwards on both those tours to allow him to get the right balance in the game the Lions played. It was there on paper, but not in the minds of the players because among the backs we always knew that, if in doubt, the forwards would always go route 1 and close the game down. The nature of rugby now is to run your socks off, do what you can, knowing that, if you can't quite make it, someone else is going to come on and take up where you left off. One of the edicts of the 1997 Lions was that the numbers on your back were only relevant at the set pieces.

The more we grasp that we have to play high-risk rugby, and become good enough to play it, the better. The 1997 Lions made a bold attempt which only faltered when we struggled for possession in the tests and were forced to rely on stonewall defence. The only problem is that in Britain, and England in particular, that sort of risk-taking is seen as being barmy. I don't think it is. Sure it's difficult and demanding, but it's also hugely enjoyable and satisfying – and that's why I play sport.

In motivational terms Geech and Fran Cotton communicated very effectively the concept of giving it everything we had in an eight-week bid for immortality, and Geech instilled in us the confidence to get away from safety-first rugby. New Zealand are better at the high-risk game than we are, and their fitness levels are probably superior, but what they should bear in mind is that the Lions were only together for a few short weeks. I hope that this time the Home Unions get the inspiration to play high-risk rugby from their players returning from the 1997 Lions.

For me, there is nothing to match the Lions. I would like to see them continue for ever, although it still intrigues me how a group of blokes touring a country for a couple of months can have such a tremendous time doing something so painful. Geech is in love with the Lions, and I'm the same. They are a one-off, and there is no greater inspiration in the British and Irish game. The Lions concept breaks down barriers and preconceptions between individuals and national-ities like nothing else.

The Lions have provided most of my best moments in rugby, but the 1997 tour will always have pride of place. Nothing I can ever do will match the achievement on this tour, even if you rolled up all the grand slams, cup finals and league titles into one. Some of the younger players on the tour won't realize yet what they've done. You are only allowed by the media to feel as good as your last game. Now, I can actually walk away feeling that I've won. I will have a smile on my face, come what may, for the rest of my career.

Appendix I

THE SQUAD

The Forwards (The Donkeys)

Props

Paul Wallace

Paul – alias 'Wally' – joined the party as a late replacement for Peter Clohessy. In some ways he looks like he's Irish, but in other ways he doesn't. He's got that really pale complexion where it looks as if he's got to keep out of the sun or he's going to burn straight away. But he's got what I'd call a cute smile, he's always quite bubbly, but what he's most notable for is the constitution of an elephant. He can really drink well in the evening and then get up and train the next day without a problem. He's got a good physique, which surprised me, he's built like a pocket-battleship, and he's got the gift of the gab as all Irishmen seem to.

Graham Rowntree

One of the Leicester boys, and a good, serious pro. He's very workman-like, trains hard and has a straight attitude. The only thing that isn't serious about him is his haircut, which has earned him the nickname 'Wiggy' at Leicester – and it's one the Lions were happy to lift.

Jason Leonard

One of my closest friends, my drinking partner and minder when we go out. A great character is 'Jase', who also goes by the name of 'The Leopard', as in 'a leopard never changes its spots'. An Eastender who loves the social side of things but, again, he trains hard. He's a good laugh to be around because he's got lots of stories and he likes taking the mickey out of people – which I always find is good value. Will Carling was in constant contact with him during the tour, leaving little bulletins on his mobile phone.

Tom Smith

'The Boston Strangler.' The quiet man of the party, this squat Scotsman was even more of a pocket-battleship than Wally. Generally one of the quietest blokes any of us had ever come across – but every now and again he jumps in with both feet. He played pool, he played cards, he played table tennis. But then again he's one of those types who could go AWOL for a couple of days and you would not miss him.

He trains very hard – he's one of Jim Telfer's protégés and has been a guinea-pig for our fitness man, Dave McLean. After the first game he was in so much pain for three or four days that we thought he might be going back home, but that sorted itself out and he had a great game against Mpumalanga. Very dynamic, explosive little player. As for the nickname, he's got the reputation for being a sleepwalker and there's a rumour that did the rounds from a previous tour that his room-mate had woken up to find himself with Tom's hands round his throat. Aaaargh!

Dai Young

Another survivor from the 1989 tour. 'Big Ted' and Scott Gibbs, his fellow Welshman and rugby-league returnee, had a common sense of mickey-taking which translated well to the rest of the party. Dai is a genuinely funny man with a sense of humour which is as dry as it gets. He had a love–hate relationship with Jim Telfer. Dai thought Jim was always on his case – 'Run to this, Dai, six inches lower, Dai' – and he didn't see too much match action in the early part of the tour. But he's a mature bloke and he took it in his stride. Jim couldn't understand his good humour through all this, confiding to Alan Tait, 'I can't make him out. He's always got a smile on his face. He must be a mischievous sod.'

Hookers

Mark Regan

He seemed to be growing by the day, did 'Ronnie'. A very popular lad, everybody took the mickey out of him because of his strong Bristol accent and his habit of calling everyone either 'Babs' or 'Skin'. But he rode it out and turned it to his advantage by having a bit of a laugh because he tells a very good story. Very determined, and enjoys the confrontation, he's one of those typical hookers – mad.

Keith Wood

I shared with 'Woody' – original, eh? – in East London. I only lasted one night with him because he snores loudly enough to take the roof off. Fortunately, Jason was prepared to swop with me and, while he moved in with Woody in the evening, I snuck in with Rob Howley and got a decent night's sleep. A lovely Irish guy, who looked after himself. He didn't go mad on the drink or social side, but very easy to get along with and chew the breeze with for half an hour. A good bloke to keep on the right side of because he was the tour judge. But, to look at him, you'd never believe he is 25, would you?

Barry Williams

On early sightings you could tell that the Welsh youngster couldn't believe he was on the trip — he actually acted as if it was a dream come true. For the first couple of weeks he looked as if he was walking on water. He worked hard in training and wasn't seen out and about too much. Known as Barry 'Three Tours' Williams after chatting as if an old pro. 'Carcass' commented memorably: 'He sounds like he's been on six tours, but he's only been around a strawberry season.'

Locks

Martin Johnson

I call him 'Rubber-Lips', but he's also known as 'The Ferengi' after the space creature in *Star Trek — The New Generation*. I always gave him a lot of stick, particularly at the beginning of the tour when he took the first two weeks of his captaincy on the sidelines recuperating from a couple of injuries after a demanding domestic season. I'd get on his case with niggling little reminders of the 'I wish we could all have a couple of weeks' holiday' variety. As captain, he had to do a lot of thinking, and tended to take his time over what he wanted to say because in such a high-profile position things can be interpreted in different ways. Sometimes you could see his mind was weighed down with detail because he was attending meetings with the management and the players and not getting too much time to himself. Overall he really impressed me. He captained the side not so much through what he said, but by the way he played. He led by example, and that's ideal for a Lions squad, because he was respected by all the players in the tour party. Johno's straight to the point, he doesn't want to colour or gloss up anything – that's Martin Johnson.

Simon Shaw

He's another of those whose nickname comes from the English habit of adding a 'y' on the end, but in other respects 'Shawsy' stands out from the crowd. He's massive. His only problem is that because he's so big it seems he almost only has to fall over to pick up an injury. Always iced-up after matches, and even after training he seemed to have an ice-pack perpetually attached to his shoulder, knee or ankle. Impressed me on the table-tennis table – he's got good co-ordination for a big man. Enjoys a beer and a chat.

Jeremy Davidson

One of the success stories of the tour. Known to one and all as 'Buzz Lightyear' because of his physical resemblance to the jut-jawed character in the animated kids' film *Toy Story*. I found it difficult to understand him half the time because he has a strong Northern Irish accent and he also tends to mumble. I think he must have had a few knocks in the mouth – in fact his whole jaw looks suspect and consequently you only get bits and pieces of sentences which you then have to try to fit together. He's a good laugh, like all the Irish lads. They are brilliant tourists, they have a good time and they make the most of things.

Doddie Weir

Before he was injured, 'George' – his real name – was one of the tour characters. He and I had a strange relationship based on one-upmanship, both of us vying to get the edge over the other with a quip here or one-liner there. But there was a mutual respect about something, although I don't know what. He was playing very well but he's a self-confessed hater of training and for that reason alone I don't know how he's managed to stay in the Scotland side for so long with Jim Telfer around. He liked a wee dram of Scotch from time to time and was one of those figures that everyone found easily approachable and was prepared to give his view on most things without putting anyone's nose out of joint. I was sorry to see him go, particularly in the way he did.

Nigel Redman

When I first heard that 'Ollie' was joining the tour it didn't really sink in. Mike Catt actually mentioned he was flying in when we were playing pool but I couldn't fathom it. I thought, 'What's he doing coming out here?' In fact, it only really registered about an hour later when I was having some physiotherapy. As he was one of the forward stalwarts during my time at Bath, I was delighted for him. Given the injury problems he had had during the season – knee and back – it was amazing he made the Argentina tour with England, let alone the Lions. When he arrived I was one of the first to congratulate him, but when Fran Cotton went to pick him up one of his first questions, being a Bath boy, was whether my reaction had been to laugh or take the mickey.

Loose Forwards

Lawrence Dallaglio

'Lol' is another guy I knock around with a lot, with him, Jason and myself often forming a trio. However, although he enjoys the social side of touring, the flip side of the coin is that he is very dedicated, keen and highly competitive – he loves success. He focuses very hard on what he has to do and played the best rugby of his life last season and carried that form into the Lions tour. He sets his standards high and gets frustrated when things both inside and outside training fail to measure up. However, he doesn't stand on ceremony and, having been captain of Wasps, if he has something to say, he says it.

Eric Miller

At 21, the baby of the squad, although he looks a bit older than that. I shared with him in Port Elizabeth and he gives the impression of being as mad as a hatter, does Eric. One minute he's here, the next minute he's there – wherever you looked he seemed to be. He didn't have a lot to say, but his one constant statement was that he didn't go out without his Lions cap on back to front like a rapper. Like all the Irish boys he wouldn't say no to the occasional beer, but he never went overboard. Although he said that merely being in the party was more than he ever expected, underpinning that was a genuine determination to make the test side.

Rob Wainwright

'The Major.' What can you say about a guy who's interested in falconry? Well, we can start off with the fantastic game he had against Mpumalanga which contradicted a pre-tour speech I heard him make at the Dorchester, where, recognizing the ferocity of the competition in the back row for test places, he said he would more than likely end up captaining the midweek side. He may have said that for public consumption, but deep down he wanted a test place. Rob enjoyed himself a lot of the time, but I got the impression he had a bit of a love affair with his own body. After training you would generally find him with his top off, and my conclusion was that either he thought he was a bit too white and needed to catch some rays or he liked showing off – I never did work out which.

Tim Rodber

Another army boy, so, in keeping with the military theme, he was dubbed 'The Brigadier'. Tim has had his critics and was determined to put the record to rights both during the Five Nations and on the Lions tour. He sets his standards high and he wanted to prove that he can perform at the top of his game consistently rather than be up and down. You could tell that he was serious, because generally when he decides occasionally to have a social evening he really goes for it. This time I never saw him the worse for drink in the first month or so – he probably didn't touch a drop. He gets on very well with Geech because of the Northampton bond, and was made captain for a couple of games. This suited him because he likes being involved and in control.

Richard Hill

If you want a view of the model pro, look no further. 'Hilda' was never with any particular group of people, but he is such an easy-going, laid-back bloke that he has no trouble mixing with anybody. He could walk into a room in which there was a group of players chatting and blend in immediately because there is nothing intense about him. He gets on with his work, does what he has to do – and does it very well. He picked up a couple of knocks but was given the time to get over them, trained strongly and appeared to enjoy himself.

Neil Back

He never ceases to amaze me. Six years ago the public perception of 'Backie' was that he was a little upstart who had a very high opinion of himself and too much to say. The British have a bit of difficulty with characters like that because they like to praise people rather than have people praise themselves first. However, he's learned from experience, not least his six-month ban for pushing referee Steve Lander. However, he had already made a favourable impression on me with the way he handled himself during the 1995 World Cup. He surprised me because he was easy to get along with, a good tourist who will mingle and mix with anybody. The way he plays the game I've got to be a fan of his because he makes the backs' job so much easier. I watched him against Mpumalanga and his work-rate was simply phenomenal – he was always there. If you hadn't seen it with your own eyes, you wouldn't have believed it. He is a very good openside whose value should never be underestimated.

Scott Quinnell

Scott likes to tell a story, and more often than not he likes to be in them. Another very easy-going individual, and a great player. He is so difficult to bring down that he always makes good yards. Had a quiet tour socially but we went out for a few beers the night before he left for home. Never really got the chance to live up to his nickname: 'Volume'.

The Backs

Scrum-Halves

Rob Howley

I called him 'Elle' after the model Elle MacPherson, otherwise known as 'The Body'. He's just rippled to kingdom come, he's got a hell of a physique on him for a small man. He must have a cast-iron metabolism because he eats crap – I've never seen anyone stuff down so much chocolate and sweets. A quiet man who admits that he doesn't go out drinking very much because if he has a few over the eight he thinks he gets a bit obnoxious. So after the game against Western Province I decided to go and have a drink with him. We had a couple of bottles of wine, but we drank them too quickly and he didn't enjoy that – but he didn't get obnoxious, quite the opposite, he was good company. He's a very talented player who carried the responsibility of being one of the key men impressively before his heart-breaking shoulder injury the week before the first test.

Austin Healey

A very lively extrovert at Leicester, not so lively with England, less lively still with the Lions. Although he would never admit it, he was in very, very good company in South Africa. Although he's not the sort of personality ever to be overawed, it's just that the depth of experience, the records and the personalities of some of the people on the tour said everything, and frankly, his own career has barely started by comparison. As a result he was fairly quiet, which was no bad thing. 'Scally' the Scouser is a very confident individual who has great self-belief. He is also one of the most competitive individuals I've ever come across, and could usually be found playing cards and always for money – he'd do anything for money. But, above all, he'd do anything to win. It didn't matter if it was go-karting, pool, table tennis, darts, he was desperate to win. Fortunately he didn't win at most of them – but it didn't stop him trying.

Matt Dawson

You tend to lose sight of where Matt's been and what he's achieved because he's had so many injury problems in recent seasons. 'Daws' is a very good player, as he showed in no uncertain terms when he got his first start against Mpumalanga. He's well-built and quite tall for a scrum-half, but he's got a good pass and all the attributes. He lost a bit of headway last season because he hardly played, but England have now got real competition at scrum-half with Matt, Austin, Kyran

Bracken and Andy Gomarsall all vying for position. If Matt thought he was lucky to have made the tour party he never showed it, and he played and trained as if to the manner born. Socially he and Austin always seemed to be thick as thieves, scheming and plotting their next move.

Fly-Halves

Paul Grayson

Off the training field 'Grays' liked to relax and have a few beers, and he probably had a few more than normal when he realized that he was losing his battle against fitness early in the tour. He was gutted that the injury came at the wrong time. Jason and myself took him out for a farewell session in Pretoria, and it was a pity we didn't get to know him better, but he wasn't on tour long enough.

Gregor Townsend

'Igor.' Outside the rugby playing and training he flitted in and out of the social scene. He liked his tennis, pool, go-karting and darts – don't know what it is about the Northampton boys but they were all so good at darts they must have a board in the changing rooms – and mixed easily. Very self-assured, carries himself well. A player who proved that he could do something magical and then disastrous within the space of a minute, so he must have acres of confidence.

Mike Catt

I said to 'Catty' before the tour that I thought he'd be on his way to South Africa sooner rather than later, so when he arrived to replace Paul Grayson I said 'told you so'. Even though he arrived too late to state a case for the first test his form for England in Argentina and during the season for Bath made him the best replacement you could get.

Centres

Allan Bateman

I got on very well with 'Batman' irrespective of the fact that we were vying for the test position at outside centre. Because he's a well-travelled, worldly individual he relates to most people and was well-liked. He was unlucky with injuries – he came out having just had a knee operation and then had a hamstring twinge. Also known as 'The Shadow' because when you're having a few beers with him another character tends to emerge. He may look a bit serious but he's capable of being very bubbly and enjoyed the 'craic'.

Will Greenwood

The only uncapped player in the party, who enjoyed the trip of his life before he was concussed in the game against Free State. Otherwise known as 'Shaggy' – as in the *Scoo-bee-do* cartoon strip – Will played some great rugby. It was always a give-away when he'd been on the grog the night after a game because his hair was all over the place, and his eyes turned to slits. He was the first tour chunder after getting in late after Mpumalanga and surprised me by branching out from the Leicester boys and joining ranks with the Irish lads. He had a ball but he also played and trained hard despite getting a couple of niggling early knocks.

Scott Gibbs

Totally motivated. Very focused when playing or training, so much so that he can be a little overexuberant. He's so physically strong that he was capable of doing real damage in training sessions, and, having twisted his ankle against Border and then been suspended for a match after being cited for a punch on his return against Northerns, the frustration really built up. 'Snake' (after the Kurt Russell character in the film *Escape from New York*) enjoys a good night out, and enjoys a droll sense of humour with his big mate, Dai Young, but he also likes his own space – which probably explains why he has a secluded house on the beach back in Wales. During the tour his girlfriend Sharon (now his wife), who was expecting, sent him a baby bible to look at. Snake was on the entertainment committee with me, John Bentley and Doddie Weir.

Alan Tait

Known as 'Pidge' – because in his early days with Scotland before going to rugby league he had a pigeon chest – he was a very good, experienced tourist, who led the circuit training in the gyms. An old pro who was the best exponent of the six-day injury I've ever come across, making miraculous strides towards full fitness before every Saturday. However, he often had the knack of being in the right place at the right time and, despite being seen as a utility back, forced his way in on the left wing for the first two tests – until sidelined by injury for the last! Pidge was also notable for being a seventies disco fan – favourite song 'Disco Inferno'.

Wings

Tony Underwood

I've known 'Carruthers' (Dick Best's tag for a public-school winger always running into touch) for a long time, and although I was impressed by his attention to detail it might have been overdone. He analysed his game consistently to see whether he could improve on the contribution he was making, and made sure that he had any moves and the lines of running he had to take off pat. Socially he's totally different from Rory, i.e. he enjoys a bottle of wine, and I've always got on very well with him even if I did rag him about the Newcastle clique which emerged oh so briefly at the beginning of the tour.

John Bentley

What can be said about 'Bentos' that he hasn't already said about himself? I found him intriguing, a great tourist, interesting to listen to and a total wind-up merchant. A standard Bentos ploy would be to get someone's name called out over the p.a. system at hotel reception and watch, sniggering, as they hung around for nothing. He wasn't doing it for public acclaim, it was just a gig for him alone. After a week we thought it was Bentley's tour because he was going to all the press conferences, interviews etc., and he got a little camcorder from the documentary crew following us which he kept shoving in our faces. He was very vocal during training and during the games – so much so that sometimes you felt like telling him to shut up – but he'd already warned you that you might get fed up and to ignore him if he upset you. A big character, a real plus.

Nick Beal

Had problems with shin splints when he arrived and had a quiet opening game, but then, like most of the side, emerged against Mpumalanga. Again, 'Bealer' was good on the dart board – coming from Northampton – and put paid to the suggestion that he might be on an early flight home with Paul Grayson by coming out of his shell both on the playing field and socially as the tour progressed.

Ieuan Evans

Apart from yours truly, Ieuan was the only other survivor from the Lions tours of 1989 and 1993. He and Jason Leonard did their best to create a mutual admiration society with their standard early morning greeting: 'You're looking good,' said one, 'You're looking good,' said the other – until Jason, looking at a bleary-eyed Ieuan, broke the tryst with a 'You're lookin' bloody awful.' Before he had to leave the tour with a groin injury after the first test he was playing as well as ever. He also handles himself very well off the pitch – he's never been mad for drink – and because of that Dai Young dubbed him 'Kool and the Gang'.

Full Backs

Tim Stimpson

A bit of a contradiction. Can be quite a deep, intense customer can 'Stimmo', very much into the mind games and psychology which is supposed to get you right for sport and for life. At Newcastle there's even a story about him communing with a pine tree when he was feeling a bit low. But he also showed a very sociable side, liked having a drink and a dance, and seemed to like almost everything there was about the tour. He had said during the Five Nations with England just how much he wanted to be a part of it. A massive man, and a quick runner, he has a tendency to dissect things and judge himself harshly. For example, after the Western Province match he goal-kicked immaculately, but was banging on about the mistakes he made in open field.

Neil Jenkins

Great goal-kicker, great laugh. He has a handful of nicknames, including 'Fruit Bat', 'Ruprecht' (as in the film *Dirty Rotten Scoundrels*) and 'Jenko'. Despite his superb discipline and confidence as a goal-kicker, which did so much to win the series, there's a funny sort of insecurity there – all I had to do was look at him and he'd come over all guilty and say, 'What?', like a kid caught with his fingers covered in chocolate. He really does enjoy the post-match 'craic', he's mad for it. Like me, he couldn't quite get used to the change of culture where going out on the toot was something to feel guilty about.

The Management

Fran Cotton (Manager)

We called him 'The Pink Salmon', because just after we arrived that was the colour he went after a couple of days in the sun in Durban. Throughout the tour Fran was first-class. He had an uncanny ability to say the right thing at the right time. He was open and prepared to listen to any of the players and, despite being a legendary player, got no further involved in training than sticking on a tracksuit. By treating us like adults, he very quickly gained the respect of the squad. He always made it crystal-clear that he was there to win but, whatever the outcome of the tour or the test series, I was confident he would back us to the hilt. He was too much of a players' manager not to.

Ian McGeechan (Coach)

'Geech' was more relaxed than he was in 1993. He worked very closely with Jim Telfer, a very strong character whom he had already coached alongside for Scotland and who subsequently had a considerable input. One of the reasons Geech was more relaxed was that, by delegating to Telfer, he had less to do with the forward coaching than in 1989 or 1993 and was able to concentrate on the backs more. Ian McGeechan is a good coach who makes a point and lets it sink in rather than ramming it down your throat. At the same time he's such an enthusiast for the game that he tends to elaborate and say the same things over twenty minutes that he has made very clear in four. Geech is one of those guys you can't help but like. He's got no airs and graces – he's big enough to take a ribbing – and he's got the respect of the players as both a coach and a former player.

Jim Telfer (Assistant Coach)

A hard-nosed Scot. He was the hardest taskmaster imaginable – and fortunately I didn't have too much to do with him as a back. He was responsible for many of the best tour quotes while beasting the forwards and, underneath it all, had a great sense of humour: 'Boys I want you to run as fast as you can, and then accelerate' was a typical Telfer saying. At a court session he was tried for these verbal excesses and given the punishment of having to stand up and sing 'Rule Britannia' – he said he only knew the dirty version – whenever there was a trigger call. It had us in stitches. He wouldn't want it to be known to anyone other than his close friends and family that he has a soft side, but we saw it on occasions all the same. One of the big characters of the tour, and well respected.

Andy Keast (Coaching Assistant)

Old 'Square Eyes' must have been bored to tears at times with all the video analysis he had to do, but his input was invaluable in his assessment of the South Africans. Good fun socially, he struck up a good friendship with Mark Davies, the physio. 'Keasty' was very much to the point in terms of what he wants from rugby and what he wants a player to do. He had virtually no coaching input other than the video compilations showing us our individual performances or, from our camera behind the posts, pointing out the strengths and weaknesses of both ourselves and the opposition. The good thing was that he kept the film shows short and sweet because he realized that most of us don't have great attention spans.

Stan Bagshaw (Baggage Man)

Stan went down well right from the start at Weybridge when he was introduced and addressed the troops on how we were going to do the laundry. He started off by trying to follow the line taken by the management and be all spit-and-polish professionalism but completely lost the plot and ended up by saying, 'Just do whatever,' after spending three minutes trying to explain where and when we should put our clothes and why. In fact, he had a physically demanding job, always up at the crack of dawn getting the kit on to trucks to get them out to the airport, and then following them to make sure they were checked in properly, and then having to chase up new orders or chase any gear that was lost or not properly cleaned. Not a job you get a lot of praise for, but 'Stan The Man' was one of the unsung heroes. He'd do anything for you. However, being a very chatty sort of bloke, he had only one failing: if you wanted something kept a secret you didn't tell Stan. There was nothing malicious about it, he didn't mean to let the cat out of the bag, it was just his nature.

Dave McLean (Fitness Adviser)

Dave loves his statistics. At one stage he gave us a sheet of paper in which he wanted us to put down our stress levels, how we were sleeping, what the colour of our urine was, what our heart rates were on waking up. You do it for about the first 24 hours and then you start making it up. You know the sort of thing – Colour of urine:

Turquoise. So, after he cottoned on to that, he started coming round once a week to do the body-fat test where you get weighed and he takes caliper measurements of the skin folds on your torso. Initially he had quite an involvement in the warm-ups and the stretches, but as the tour went on he spent more time on injury rehabilitation. The fitness guys at all clubs tend to get a bit of stick, and Dave was no exception. He only lost his rag once – Will Greenwood was mucking about when Dave had his electronic timer out and was testing our speed over different distances – which spoke volumes for his self-control.

Mark Davies (Physiotherapist)

For his age he's still in pretty good nick, so the Welsh boys called him 'Carcass'. He was a scream – because of his seventies-style soccer-star haircut, he and Andy Keast, who he used to go on recces with whenever we got to a new port of call, were known also as 'Rodney Marsh and George Best' – and he loved the banter and interaction with the players. A former Welsh international back rower, Carcass has had the bridge of his nose smashed flat at some stage with the result that he speaks in a very nasal way. If that wasn't bad enough, his South Walian twang is rendered virtually incomprehensible because he insists on talking out of the side of his mouth like some great conspirator. A good impressionist could have a field day with Carcass.

Bob Burrows (Media Liaison Officer)

Bob worked behind the scenes at management meetings and, more publicly, organising post-match functions and tour press conferences, always wrapping up with the words 'Well that's it folks.' Bob – also known as the Chardonnay Kid because of his taste in fine wines – got a lot of stick from the squad although in fairness he didn't have the greatest job with which to make an impression.

Samantha Peters

'Sam' was meant to be Fran Cotton's PA but appeared to all of us to end up as Bob's. She got on with her job and mingled in so well that we forgot there was a woman on the trip – and I mean that as a compliment. You could almost see the relief on her face at the end of the day, thinking thank heavens that's over, oh no, there's Bob, better go and hide. However, she put herself up for the job and she also made the most of it. For a few of the support staff it was probably harder work than they imagined – and Sam could be numbered among them.

James Robson (Doctor)

'Robbo' was well respected, very chatty when you went into the medical room and was on call 24 hours a day. If anything he was probably over-cautious and gave the worst-case scenario when there were injuries. He never hung around when it came to getting people

X-rayed or MRI-scanned, or seeking a second opinion. Very thorough, very competent and left nothing to chance.

Richard Wegrzyk (Masseur)

I knew Richard (or 'The Painless Pole') because he is the England masseur and I warned him before the tour that he didn't know what he was letting himself in for. I told him that he would be at the beck and call of anyone who was at a loose end and might just fancy a massage. Sometimes you saw him walking around with a stack of towels and his eyes popping out of his head where he'd O/D'd on the fumes from his oils. He's also an acupuncturist and he used that on anything from strains to scrum-pox. I went to him a couple of times when I wanted to really relax and he stuck needles in my ankles, hands and knees. I nodded off for 20 minutes and woke up feeling refreshed. However, where the workload was concerned, he can't say I didn't warn him.

Dave Alred (Kicking Coach)

We always called him 'Hank the Yank' when he did some kicking coaching at Bath – where he had also played – because of his American football background. On this tour, however, he was dubbed 'All Head'. When I first came across him three or four years ago he was full of all the regimentation bullshit from American football where you all line up like kids to be put through your paces, and he seemed to set great store by people being kitted out properly. Mind you, he is always immaculately turned out himself. As a kicking coach, which is what he was in South Africa for, he gets results, as his work on tour with Gregor Townsend and Tim Stimpson testified. He is a great enthusiast and was decent enough to tell me how pleased he was that I was playing well after my disappointments with England. All the backs did the 'little and often' kicking drills he prescribed and he also had a hand in the pre-training warm-ups where Ronnie Regan used to take the mickey out of him something rotten. 'When are you going to turn the page, Dave?' was Ronnie's favourite cat-call.

Appendix 2

TOUR RECORD

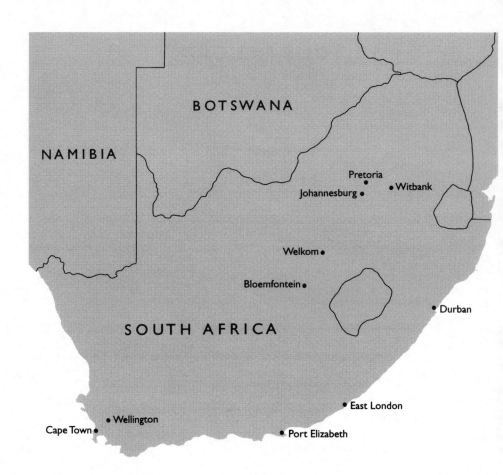

TOUR ITINERARY

1   24 May v **Eastern Province Invitational XV**
PORT ELIZABETH

2   28 May v **Border**
EAST LONDON

3   31 May v **Western Province**
CAPE TOWN

4   4 June v **Mpumalanga**
WITBANK

5   7 June v **Northern Transvaal**
PRETORIA

6   11 June v **Gauteng**
JOHANNESBURG

7   14 June v **Natal**
DURBAN

8   17 June v **Emerging Springboks**
WELLINGTON

9   21 June v **South Africa** FIRST TEST
CAPE TOWN

10   24 June v **Free State**
BLOEMFONTEIN

11   28 June v **South Africa** SECOND TEST
DURBAN

12   1 July v **Northern Free State**
WELKOM

13   5 July v **South Africa** THIRD TEST
JOHANNESBURG

TOUR RECORD

Played	13
Won	11
Drawn	0
Lost	2
Points for	480
Points against	278

APPEARANCES

8

Back (1 as replacement)   **Bentley**   **Davidson** (1)   **Jenkins** (2)
Leonard (3)   **Underwood** (1)   **Wainwright** (1)

7

Bateman (1)   **Dallaglio**   **Guscott**   **Healey** (3)
Smith   **Shaw** (1)   **Stimpson** (1)

6

Catt (1)   **Dawson** (2)   **Gibbs** (1)   **Greenwood** (1)
Johnson   **Regan** (1)   **Rowntree** (1)   **Tait** (1)
Townsend   **Wallace** (1)   **Young** (2)

5

Beal   **Evans**   **Hill**   **Miller** (1)
Rodber   **Wood**

4

Howley   **Redman**   **Williams** (1)

3

Quinnell (1)   **Weir**

2

Diprose

1

Bracken   **Grayson**   **Stanger**

POINTS SCORERS

111

Stimpson (4 Tries, 23 Conversions, 15 Penalties)

110

Jenkins (2T, 17C, 22P)

35

Bentley (7T)   **Underwood** (7T)

23

Guscott (4T, 1 Drop Goal)

20

Beal (4T)   **Wainwright** (4T)

15

Dawson (3T)   **Evans** (3T)

13

Catt (2T, 1P)   **Townsend** (2T, 1DG)

10

Regan (2T)   **Shaw** (2T)   **Tait** (2T)

5

Back (1T)   **Bateman** (1T)   **Bracken** (1T)   **Dallaglio** (1T)
Greenwood (1T)   **Healey** (1T)   **Rowntree** (1T)   **Weir** (1T)

E. PROVINCE INV. XV		BRITISH ISLES
T. van Rensburg	15	N. Jenkins
D. Keyser	14	I. Evans (T. Underwood 67 min)
R. van Jaarsveld	13	J. Guscott
H. le Roux	12	W. Greenwood
H. Pedro	11	N. Beal
K. Ford (R. Fouie 42 min)	10	G. Townsend
C. Alcock	9	R. Howley
D. Saayman	1	T. Smith
J. Kirsten (capt)	2	K. Wood (B. Williams 67 min)
W. Enslin (W. Lessing 40 min)	3	J. Leonard (capt)
K. Wiese	4	S. Shaw (J. Davidson 71 min)
A. Du Preez	5	D. Weir
M. Webber (M. van de Merwe 42 min)	6	L. Dallaglio
S. Scott-Young	7	R. Hill
J. Greeff	8	S. Quinnell

Scorers

D. Keyser (T) 5	J. Guscott (2T) 10
T. van Rensburg (2P) 6	D. Weir (T) 5
	T. Underwood (T) 5
	W. Greenwood (T) 5
	N. Jenkins (4C, 2P) 14

E. PROVINCE INV. XV   11–39   BRITISH ISLES

BORDER		BRITISH ISLES
R. Bennett	15	T. Stimpson
K. Hilton-Green	14	J. Bentley
G. Hechter	13	A. Bateman
K. Molotana (D. Maidza 45 min)	12	S. Gibbs (A. Tait 45 min)
A. Claasen	11	T. Underwood
G. Miller	10	P. Grayson
J. Bradbrook	9	A. Healey (M. Dawson 55 min)
H. Kok	1	G. Rowntree
R. van Zyl (capt)	2	M. Regan
D. du Preez	3	D. Young (P. Wallace 68 min)
M. Swart	4	R. Wainwright
S. Botha	5	G. Weir
J. Gehring (L. Blakeway 74 min)	6	J. Davidson
A. Botha (D. Coetzer 80 min)	7	N. Back
A. Fox	8	E. Miller

Scorers

A. Claasen (T) 5	J. Bentley (T) 5
G. Miller (3P) 9	M. Regan (T) 5
	R. Wainwright (T) 5
	T. Stimpson (P) 3

BORDER   14–18   BRITISH ISLES

WESTERN PROVINCE		BRITISH ISLES
J. Swart	15	T. Stimpson
J. Small	14	I. Evans
R. Fleck	13	A. Tait (W. Greenwood 72 min)
R. Muir (P. Koen 57–64 min) (capt)	12	J. Guscott
S. Berridge	11	J. Bentley
P. Montgomery	10	G. Townsend
S. Hatley	9	R. Howley
G. Pagel (T. van der Linde 57 min)	1	G. Rowntree
A. Paterson	2	B. Williams
K. Andrews	3	J. Leonard
F. van Heerden	4	M. Johnson (capt)
H. Louw	5	S. Shaw
C. Krige (R. Skinstad 64 min)	6	L. Dallaglio
R. Brink	7	R. Hill
A. Aitken	8	T. Rodber (S. Quinnell 62 min)

Scorers

R. Muir (2T) 10	J. Bentley (2T) 10
R. Brink (T) 5	A. Tait (T) 5
P. Montgomery (3C) 6	I. Evans (T) 5
	T. Stimpson (3C, 4P) 18

WESTERN PROVINCE   21–38   BRITISH ISLES

MPUMALANGA		BRITISH ISLES
E. von Gericke	15	N. Beal
J. Visagie	14	I. Evans
R. Potgieter	13	A. Bateman
G. Gendall	12	W. Greenwood
P. Nel (A. van Rooyen 78 min)	11	T. Underwood
R. van As	10	N. Jenkins
D. van Zyl	9	M. Dawson
H. Swart	1	T. Smith
H. Kemp	2	K. Wood (M. Regan 53 min)
A. Botha	3	P. Wallace (D. Young 75 min)
F. Rossouw	4	R. Wainwright
E. van der Berg	5	D. Weir (S. Shaw 57)
M. Bosman	6	J. Davidson
P. Joubert	7	N. Back
T. Oosthuizen (J. Beukes 72 min)	8	T. Rodber

Scorers

Joubert (2T) 14	Wainwright (3T) 15
van As (2C) 4	Evans (2T) 14
	Underwood (2T) 14
	Dawson (T) 7
	Jenkins (T, 7C) 19
	Beal (T) 7

MPUMALANGA   14–64   BRITISH ISLES

NORTHERN TRANSVAAL

BRITISH ISLES

NORTHERN TRANSVAAL		BRITISH ISLES
G. Bouwer	15	T. Stimpson
W. Lourens (G. Esterhuizen 34 min)	14	J. Bentley (S. Gibbs 60 min)
J. Schutte	13	J. Guscott
D. van Schalkwyk	12	A. Tait
C. Steyn	11	T. Underwood
R. de Marigny	10	G. Townsend
C. Breytenbach	9	R. Howley
L. Campher	1	G. Rowntree
H. Tromp (J. Brooks 63 min)	2	M. Regan
P. Boer (M. Proudfoot 70 min)	3	J. Leonard (D. Young 74 min)
D. Grobbelaar (G. Laufs 39 min)	4	M. Johnson (capt)
D. Badenhorst	5	S. Shaw
N. van der Walt (R. Schroeder 63 min)	6	L. Dallaglio
S. Bekker	7	E. Miller
A. Richter (capt)	8	S. Quinnell

Scorers

C. Steyn (T, 3C, 3P) 20
D. van Schalkwyk (2T) 10
A. Richter (T) 5

J. Guscott (2T) 10
G. Townsend (T) 5
T. Stimpson (3C, 3P) 15

NORTHERN TRANSVAAL   35–30   BRITISH ISLES

GAUTENG LIONS		BRITISH ISLES
D. du Toit	15	N. Beal
J. Gillingham	14	J. Bentley
J. van der Walt	13	J. Guscott
H. Le Roux	12	W. Greenwood
P. Hendricks	11	T. Underwood (N. Jenkins 57 min)
L. van Rensburg	10	M. Catt
J. Roux	9	A. Healey
R. Grau	1	T. Smith
C. Rossouw (J. Dalton 52 min)	2	B. Williams
K. van Greuning (B. Swart 60 min)	3	P. Wallace
K. Wiese (capt)	4	N. Redman
B. Thorne	5	J. Davidson
A. Vos	6	R. Wainwright
P. Krause	7	N. Back
W. Brosnihan	8	T. Rodber

Scorers

A. Vos (T) 5   A. Healey (T) 5
D. du Toit (3P) 9   J. Bentley (T) 5
                      N. Jenkins (2C, P) 7
                      M. Catt (P) 3

NATAL		BRITISH ISLES
G. Lawless	15	N. Jenkins
S. Payne	14	I. Evans
J. Thomson	13	A. Bateman (M. Catt 65 min)
P. Muller	12	S. Gibbs
J. Joubert	11	A. Tait
H. Scriba	10	G. Townsend
R. du Preez	9	R. Howley (M. Dawson 12 min)
O. Le Roux	1	T. Smith (J. Leonard 67 min)
J. Allan	2	K. Wood
R. Kempson	3	D. Young
J. Slade	4	M. Johnson (capt)
N. Wegner	5	S. Shaw
W. van Heerden (R. Strudwick 42 min)	6	L. Dallaglio
W. Fyvie (capt)	7	R. Hill
D. Kriese	8	E. Miller

Scorers

G. Lawless (4P) 12	G. Townsend (T, DG) 8
	M. Catt (T) 5
	L. Dallaglio (T) 5
	N. Jenkins (3C, 6P) 24

NATAL   12–42   BRITISH ISLES

EMERGING SPRINGBOKS

M. Smith (K. Malotana 62 min)	15	T. Stimpson
D. Keyser	14	J. Bentley
P. Montgomery	13	A. Bateman
M. Hendricks	12	W. Greenwood
P. Treu	11	N. Beal
L. van Rensburg (M. Goosen 21 min)	10	M. Catt
J. Adlam (K. Myburgh 11 min)	9	A. Healey
R. Kempson (L. Campher 65 min)	1	G. Rowntree
D. Santon (J. Brooks 67 min)	2	M. Regan
N. du Toit	3	J. Leonard (capt)
W. Brosnihan (T. Arendse 71 min)	4	N. Redman
R. Opperman	5	J. Davidson
B. Els	6	R. Wainwright
P. Smit	7	N. Back
J. Coetzee	8	A. Diprose

BRITISH ISLES

Scorers

W. Brosnihan (T) 5	N. Beal (3T) 15
M. Goosen (T) 5	G. Rowntree (T) 5
P. Treu (T) 5	T. Stimpson (T, 6C, 3P) 26
M. Smith (C, P) 5	M. Catt (T) 5
P. Montgomery (C) 2	

EMERGING SPRINGBOKS   22–51   BRITISH ISLES

SOUTH AFRICA		BRITISH ISLES
A. Joubert	15	N. Jenkins
J. Small	14	I. Evans
J. Mulder	13	S. Gibbs
E. Lubbe (R. Bennett 41 min)	12	J. Guscott
A. Snyman	11	A. Tait
H. Honiball	10	G. Townsend
J. van der Westhuizen	9	M. Dawson
O. du Randt	1	T. Smith (J. Leonard 78 min)
N. Drotske	2	K. Wood
A. Garvey	3	P. Wallace
M. Andrews	4	M. Johnson (capt)
H. Strydom	5	J. Davidson
R. Kruger	6	L. Dallaglio
A. Venter	7	R. Hill
G. Teichmann (capt)	8	T. Rodber

Scorers

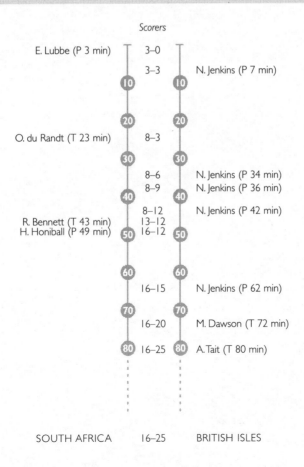

E. Lubbe (P 3 min)	3–0	
	3–3	N. Jenkins (P 7 min)
O. du Randt (T 23 min)	8–3	
	8–6	N. Jenkins (P 34 min)
	8–9	N. Jenkins (P 36 min)
	8–12	N. Jenkins (P 42 min)
R. Bennett (T 43 min)	13–12	
H. Honiball (P 49 min)	16–12	
	16–15	N. Jenkins (P 62 min)
	16–20	M. Dawson (T 72 min)
	16–25	A. Tait (T 80 min)

SOUTH AFRICA	16–25	BRITISH ISLES

FREE STATE		BRITISH ISLES
M.J. Smith	15	T. Stimpson
J. van Wyk	14	J. Bentley
H. Muller (capt)	13	W. Greenwood (N. Jenkins 40 min)
B. Venter	12	A. Bateman
S. Brink	11	T. Underwood
J. de Beer	10	M. Catt
S. Fourie	9	A. Healey
D. Groenewald	1	G. Rowntree (J. Leonard 73 min)
C. Marais	2	B. Williams
W. Meyer	3	D. Young
R. Opperman	4	N. Redman (capt)
B. Els	5	S. Shaw
C. van Rensberg	6	R. Wainwright
J. Erasmus	7	N. Back
J. Coetzee	8	E. Miller

Scorers

S. Brink (2T) 10	T. Stimpson (T, 4C, 3P) 22
J. de Beer (T, 3C, 3P) 20	J. Bentley (3T) 15
	A. Bateman (T) 5
	N. Jenkins (T) 5
	T. Underwood (T) 5

FREE STATE   30–52   BRITISH ISLES

SOUTH AFRICA		BRITISH ISLES
A. Joubert	15	N. Jenkins
A. Snyman	14	J. Bentley
P. Montgomery	13	S. Gibbs
D. van Schalkwyk	12	J. Guscott
P. Rossouw	11	A. Tait (A. Healey 75 min)
H. Honiball	10	G. Townsend
J. van der Westhuizen	9	M. Dawson
O. du Randt	1	T. Smith
N. Drotske	2	K. Wood
A. Garvey	3	P. Wallace
H. Strydom	4	M. Johnson (capt)
M. Andrews	5	J. Davidson
R. Kruger (F. van Heerden 50 min)	6	L. Dallaglio
A. Venter	7	R. Hill (N. Back 56 min)
G. Teichmann (capt)	8	T. Rodber (E. Miller 77 min)

Scorers

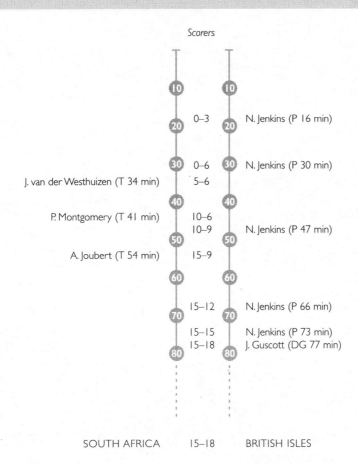

	0–3	N. Jenkins (P 16 min)
	0–6	N. Jenkins (P 30 min)
J. van der Westhuizen (T 34 min)	5–6	
P. Montgomery (T 41 min)	10–6	
	10–9	N. Jenkins (P 47 min)
A. Joubert (T 54 min)	15–9	
	15–12	N. Jenkins (P 66 min)
	15–15	N. Jenkins (P 73 min)
	15–18	J. Guscott (DG 77 min)

SOUTH AFRICA   15–18   BRITISH ISLES

NORTHERN FREE STATE		BRITISH ISLES
M. Ehrentraut (J. Burrows 67 min)	15	**T. Stimpson**
R. Harmse	14	**A. Stanger**
A. van Buuren	13	**A. Bateman**
T. de Beer	12	**N. Beal**
W. Nagel	11	**T. Underwood**
E. Herbert	10	**M. Catt**
J. Jerling (capt)	9	**K. Bracken** (A. Healey 54 min)
K. Appelgryn	1	**J. Leonard (capt)** (G. Rowntree 40 min)
O. Wagener (C. Dippenaar 78 min)	2	**M. Regan**
B. Nel	3	**D. Young**
H. Kershaw	4	**N. Redman**
K. Heydenrich	5	**S. Shaw**
S. Nieuwenhuyzen	6	**R. Wainwright**
E. Delport (A. Fouche 75 min)	7	**N. Back**
M. Venter	8	**A. Diprose**

Scorers

M. Ehrentraut (T) 5	T. Underwood (3T) 15
O. Wagener (T) 5	T. Stimpson (2T, 7C, P) 27
T. de Beer (T) 5	S. Shaw (2T) 10
E. Herbert (T, 4C, 2P) 19	N. Back (T) 5
penalty try 5	K. Bracken (T) 5
	M. Regan (T) 5

NORTHERN FREE STATE   39–67   BRITISH ISLES

SOUTH AFRICA

Player	No.
R. Bennett	15
A. Snyman	14
P. Montgomery (H. Honiball 53 min)	13
D. van Schalkwyk	12
P. Rossouw	11
J. de Beer (J. Swart 71 min)	10
J. van der Westhuizen (W. Swanepoel 81 min)	9
P. du Randt (A. Garvey 63 min)	1
J. Dalton (N. Drotske 69 min)	2
D. Theron	3
H. Strydom	4
K. Otto	5
J. Erasmus	6
A. Venter	7
G. Teichmann (F. van Heerden 73 min)	8

BRITISH ISLES

No.	Player
15	N. Jenkins
14	J. Bentley
13	J. Guscott (A. Bateman 40 min)
12	S. Gibbs
11	T. Underwood (T. Stimpson 28 min)
10	M. Catt
9	M. Dawson (A. Healey 82 min)
1	T. Smith
2	M. Regan
3	P. Wallace
4	M. Johnson (capt)
5	J. Davidson
6	R. Wainwright
7	N. Back
8	L. Dallaglio

Scorers

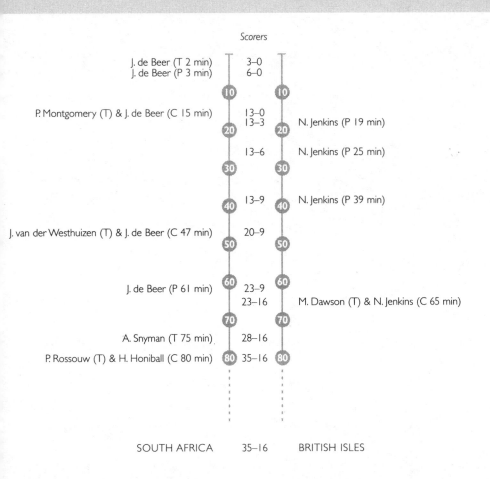

South Africa	Score	British Isles
J. de Beer (T 2 min)	3–0	
J. de Beer (P 3 min)	6–0	
P. Montgomery (T) & J. de Beer (C 15 min)	13–0	
	13–3	N. Jenkins (P 19 min)
	13–6	N. Jenkins (P 25 min)
	13–9	N. Jenkins (P 39 min)
J. van der Westhuizen (T) & J. de Beer (C 47 min)	20–9	
J. de Beer (P 61 min)	23–9	
	23–16	M. Dawson (T) & N. Jenkins (C 65 min)
A. Snyman (T 75 min)	28–16	
P. Rossouw (T) & H. Honiball (C 80 min)	35–16	

SOUTH AFRICA	35–16	BRITISH ISLES